Cambridge Collections

Happy families?

a collection of fiction and non-fiction

Edited by Chris Buckton
Series editor: Michael Marland

CAMBRIDGE UNIVERSITY PRESS
Cambridge, New York, Melbourne, Madrid, Cape Town, Singapore,
São Paulo, Delhi

Cambridge University Press
The Edinburgh Building, Cambridge CB2 8RU, UK

www.cambridge.org
Information on this title: www.cambridge.org/9780521730860

© Cambridge University Press 2008

This publication is in copyright. Subject to statutory exception and to the provisions of relevant collective licensing agreements, no reproduction of any part may take place without the written permission of Cambridge University Press.

First published 2008

Printed in the United Kingdom at the University Press, Cambridge

A catalogue record for this publication is available from the British Library

ISBN 978-0-521-73086-0 paperback

Cover image: Michael Cogliantry/The Image Bank/Getty Images
Cover design by Smith
Illustrations by Tom Sperling/The Bright Agency

Cambridge University Press has no responsibility for the persistence or accuracy of URLs for external or third-party Internet websites referred to in this publication, and does not guarantee that any content on such websites is, or will remain, accurate or appropriate. Information regarding prices, travel timetables and other factual information given in this work are correct at the time of first printing but Cambridge University Press does not guarantee the accuracy of such information thereafter.

Contents

General introduction   vii

1 Celebration and security   1

My House   2
Annette Mbaye d'Erneville

An Overcrowded House   3
Adèle Geras

Ramadan: Why Muslim Families Fast   10
Kiran Ansari

Family Forum: Our Family Mealtimes Are Battlegrounds   15
Guardian readers' letters

A Gentleman's Agreement   19
Elizabeth Jolley

My Parents   26
Adrian Mitchell

Forging a Family   29
Sue Palmer

A Christmas Carol   33
Charles Dickens

The Trouble Was Meals   39
Elizabeth Bennett

Activities   42

2 Conflict and confusion   49

Buried Treasure   50
Chris Buckton

A Parents' and Teenagers' Alphabet Book   61
David Crystal

Urgent Note to My Parents   63
Hiawyn Oram

One Small Step   64
Shyama Perera

Independence   78
Anne Frank

Getting the Messages   83
Anne Fine

Family Values   93
Richard Benson

She's Leaving Home   100
The Beatles

Romeo and Juliet   102
William Shakespeare

Activities   107

3 Change and uncertainty   117

Lost and Found   118
Rachel Anderson

A Family Photo   122
Lynette Craig

Two of Everything   123
Jackie Kay

Saturday Fathers   124
Kit and the Widow

New Families: the Experience of Divorce   126

The Ultimate Safari   130
Nadine Gordimer

Me, a Mother at 15? No Way!   142
Jeremy Hart

The Sorrows of Sandra Saint   148
Lee Hall

Compass and Torch Elizabeth Baines	164
An Ideal Family Katherine Mansfield	172
Activities	181

4 History and continuity — 189

Two poems Judith Nicholls	190
From the Grave to the Cradle Hugh Cunningham	193
Little Brother Mary Mann	196
Keeping Mum Sara Selvarajah	202
Oral Tradition Carolyn Steele Agosta	204
When Ma and Pa Kept Control Thea Thompson	214
The Kitchen David Almond	220
Patterned Ways Jo Hilton	227
Follower Seamus Heaney	229
Heredity Thomas Hardy	231
Activities	232
Notes on authors	**241**
Acknowledgements	246

General introduction

Most people have some experience of family as they grow up, either as a member or as an individual looking in from outside. This anthology expresses that experience through poetry, fiction, plays, interviews, diaries and letters. It presents families in all their variety, now and in the past, and reflects a wide range of cultures and settings. The question mark in the title is there for a reason. Family life generally brings plenty of pleasures but sometimes it can feel like a prison, particularly when you are in your teens. So as well as celebrating the good times, this collection confronts some of the conflicts too, and explores changing family structures caused by such events as social upheaval, separation or old age.

The subject of families can be a difficult one to tackle at a time when there can be no single, simple agreement about what family life should be like. But the many differences represented here can help to broaden everyone's understanding. We all have to struggle to find our own values and decide what kind of family we might want to make for ourselves. I hope that this book will help you to share your own experiences of family life and to think about its pleasures, pains and failures; to challenge your own and others' assumptions; and perhaps to work towards a definition of what 'family' means to you.

The anthology is divided into four themes, although there are many overlaps. Sometimes I have chosen several pieces to illustrate a sub-theme, such as family meals, or falling out with each other, or following in parents' footsteps, so that you can compare different viewpoints.

Within each section, the more difficult texts are placed at the end. To support your reading, certain words (these are numbered) in the texts are explained in the footnotes. Ideas for further reading accompany each text, and notes about the authors can be found at the end of the anthology. Each section concludes with a range of reading, writing, speaking, listening and drama activities to help you explore and enjoy the authors' ideas, opinions, style, language and techniques.

The text-specific activities pages are divided into the following activity types: *Before you read* (pre-reading stimulation activities), *What's it about?* (comprehension-style questions) and *Thinking about the text* (activities which move beyond the text itself). At the very end of each section, a series of *Compare and contrast* activities provide opportunities to compare two or more texts.

The first section, *Celebration and security*, looks at times of warmth and closeness: forging family links, supporting each other through hard times, sharing beliefs, or celebrating special occasions. These pieces should help you to explore the strength of family bonds and maybe compare different beliefs with your own.

The second section, *Conflict and confusion*, is about the times when the needs of different members of the family are in headlong collision, when feelings are muddled and often contradictory. Reading about the emotional experiences of others can often help to bring insight into your own conflicts and gives you a chance to reflect on the reasons for family disagreements.

The third section, *Change and uncertainty*, focuses on those times when the family is torn apart by war, by parents separating, or by children growing up.

The fourth section, *History and continuity*, looks at some of the different expectations of family life over the centuries, as well as the elements that don't change: for instance, customs and physical likenesses passed down through generations. How much do you know about your own family history? And who do you 'take after'?

In choosing the pieces, I have tried to keep a balance between cultures, gender, historical periods, and literary genres. But most of all I wanted each text to involve you, to get you thinking about your own life, talking, discussing, agreeing or disagreeing, and explaining why you react as you do.

Chris Buckton

1 Celebration and security

God bless us every one!

We're starting with the positives! This section explores the moments when the family comes together, whether it's at mealtimes (not always harmonious . . .), sharing interests and activities, or helping each other out when the going gets rough. The security that a family provides can make a huge difference to our well-being, but sometimes it's taken for granted and we forget how vital our parents' love for us is.

Activities

1 In a small group, brainstorm a list of all the positive things about a family. No negatives allowed!

2 Think of a time when you particularly valued your family – perhaps a time when someone was there when you really needed them, or when you felt proud of them for some reason. Write a short piece, singing their praises.

3 Look through some newspapers or magazines and cut out any items that celebrate the family – maybe a tale of bravery, or family activity, or just an announcement among the small ads. (Local newspapers are often more positive than the national press. Why do you think this is?)

My House

by Annette Mbaye d'Erneville

> Annette Mbaye d'Erneville comes from Senegal in Africa. This poem is part of a section called 'Love and Celebrations' in an anthology of African poetry.

I have built my house
Without sand, without water
My mother's heart
Forms a great wall
My father's arms
The floor and the roof
My sister's laughter
The doors and the windows
My brother's eyes
Light up the house
My home feels good
My home is sweet

Further reading

My House comes from an anthology of African poetry called *Talking Drums* (Bloomsbury Publishing PLC, 2004). It covers themes such as nature, animals, death and national turmoil as well as poems about family love.

If you enjoyed this poem, you might also like the work of Charles Mungoshi, a poet from Zimbabwe. His collection is called *The Milkman Doesn't Only Deliver Milk* (Baobab Books, 1998).

An Overcrowded House
by Adèle Geras

> In *An Overcrowded House* Adèle Geras weaves together a traditional Jewish folk tale with memories of her much-loved grandmother.

In the entrance hall of my grandmother's flat, there was a cupboard set so high up in the wall that only a tall person standing on a chair could open it. Luckily, my grandmother needed what was kept up there once a year only, so it had to be reached on two occasions: once, to bring out the Passover dishes ready for the Festival, every spring, and the second time to put them all away for another twelve months. My tallest cousin, Arieh, was always the person who had to stand on the chair and pass down dishes and cups and plates, knives and forks and pots and pans and glasses to my grandmother and me, waiting to carry them to the kitchen.

A Jewish Passover celebration.

At Passover time, all the ordinary dishes were put away and the whole flat was cleaned from top to bottom. Not a single crumb was allowed to lurk forgotten in the corner. Holes in the wall had to be plastered over. Sometimes, my grandmother decided that this or that room needed whitewashing, and she would pile all the furniture into the middle of the room for a day, and cover it with sheets, and then slap a thick, white sloppy brush up and down the walls.

'Why do you have the best things hidden away in the cupboard all the time?' I asked my grandmother. 'Why are they only allowed down into the house for a week?'

'Because it's a special celebration,' said my grandmother. 'It's to celebrate the escape of the Jews from their captivity in Egypt. We will read the whole story again, on the night of the First Seder.'[1]

For the Seder the door between the dining-room and the room where the long, blue sofa was, was folded back, and the table was pulled out to its full length. More than twenty people would sit around it for the Passover meal, eating matzos[2] and bitter herbs and drinking sweet wine, and telling the story of the Plagues that God sent down to the land of Egypt. In the Hagadah, the book we looked at as the meal continued, there were coloured drawings of the Plagues: frogs, locusts, boils, and a very frightening picture showing a dead child covered in blood, and representing the Death of the First Born. There was also a picture of Moses parting the Red Sea, with high, blue waves towering above the heads of the Israelites like walls of sapphire. We sang songs, and waited up till late at night to see whether this year, the prophet Elijah would come and drink the glass of wine my grandmother always put out for him. At the end of the meal, my cousins and I would run all over the flat

---

[1]**First Seder**   a ceremonial meal held on the first night of Passover; Passover celebrates the deliverance of the Israelites from Slavery in Egypt
[2]**matzos**   unleavened bread (made without yeast or soda), traditional Passover food

searching for the Afikoman. This was half a matzo, wrapped in a napkin, which my grandmother hid like a treasure. Whoever found it won a small prize: an apple or a square of chocolate. There were so many cousins rushing about that I never managed to find the Afikoman, but my grandmother gave us all apples and chocolate too, so I didn't mind.

'It's not very fair for the winner, though,' I said to my grandmother. 'It makes winning less special.'

'Nonsense,' said my grandmother. 'Finding the Afikoman is an honour and it brings good luck. And looking all over the place is fun, too.'

In spite of the special dishes, and the book with pictures of the Plagues, in spite of the sips of sweet wine and the brown-freckled matzos which tasted so delicious with strawberry jam on them, I was always quite glad when the festival was over and the visitors went home. Then I could have my grandmother to myself again and she could tell me stories.

'You don't know,' she said, 'how well off you are. I should tell you the story of Mordechai and Chaya. Once upon a time, there was a farmer called Mordechai, who lived in a miserable little farmhouse right on the edge of the village. He had two muddy fields next to the house, where he tried to grow this and that and the other. I have to tell you that most of the time he failed miserably, and when Chaya took the farm produce to the market and set it out on a stall, people walked by with their noses in the air saying: "Pshaw! Such cabbages I wouldn't feed to my chickens! Do you call this a turnip? This is a turnip's wizened grandfather! And this is not a potato, this is a joke . . ." and so forth. But Chaya didn't laugh. The money grew scarcer and scarcer, and the couple grew more and more miserable. Then, one terrible day, Mordechai's father died, leaving Mordechai's mother penniless. She had to sell her house to pay her late husband's debts, and so there she was, homeless at her age. Well, there was no alternative: the poor old lady had to move in at once with Mordechai and Chaya. It was difficult to know quite where to put her. The farmhouse was really two rooms: one large room, with a corner curtained off to hide the bed where Mordechai and Chaya slept, and one tiny room which the couple called the kitchen, but which could more accurately have been called a cupboard with a window. When Mordechai's mother moved in, he hung a curtain across another corner of the large room, to hide the bed she had brought with her, and tried to make the best of it. But it was difficult.

"What shall we do?" he asked Chaya. "She snores at night and keeps me awake."

"She squeezes into the kitchen to help me cook," said Chaya, "so that I can hardly move. I think you should go and see the Rabbi. Ask his advice."

"What good will that do?" asked Mordechai.

"What harm will it do?" his wife replied.

So in the end, Mordechai went to the Rabbi and told him all his troubles. This rabbi was not as clever as Rabbi Samuels, but he wasn't a fool. He listened to Mordechai, and muttered and mumbled into his beard, and fixed his eyes on an interesting spot on the ceiling, and finally he turned to Mordechai.

"Have you any livestock?" he asked.

"A few chickens . . . a goat . . . a cow to give milk . . . nothing much, I assure you."

"Take the chickens," said the Rabbi, "and move them into the house with you."

"Into the house?" Mordechai thought the Rabbi had gone mad.

"Exactly," said the Rabbi, "do as I say and your troubles will soon be over."

Mordechai did as the Rabbi said. Never had he and Chaya been so miserable. The chickens squawked all day and got under everyone's feet. They laid eggs in unexpected places and flew on to the table at mealtimes to share what little food there was. The rooster had decided that Mordechai and Chaya's brass bedstead was his perch, and there, every morning he would split the dawn in half with his crowing. Mordechai and Chaya used to leap out of their skins in fright.

"Go back to the Rabbi," said Chaya. "Tell him everything is ten times worse than before."

So Mordechai went and poured out all his woes to the Rabbi. The Rabbi muttered and mumbled into his beard and fixed his eyes on an interesting spot on the back of the door, and then finally he turned to Mordechai.

"You said you had a cow?" he asked.

"Yes . . . one cow."

"Bring the cow into the house," said the Rabbi.

"Where will I put her?"

"Tie her up to the handle of the door," said the Rabbi. "All your troubles will soon be over."

Mordechai returned to the farmhouse and told his wife what the Rabbi had said.

"He has taken leave of his senses," said Chaya. "But he is an educated man, so we should at least try it."

Life immediately went from bad to worse. No one could move in or out of the door without bumping into the cow. Twice, she pulled the rickety door off its hinges, and once chewed up both the curtain hiding Mordechai's mother's bed and some of her blankets as well.

"Go back to the Rabbi," said Chaya after a week had passed. "Tell him everything is a hundred times worse than before."

So Mordechai went and cried out his anguish to the Rabbi. The Rabbi muttered and mumbled into his beard and fixed his eyes on an interesting spot on the floor and then finally he turned to Mordechai.

"Do you still have a goat?"

"Yes . . . one goat."

"Bring the goat into the house."

"Where will I put him?"

"Tie him up to the end of your bed," said the Rabbi, "and your troubles will soon be over."

Mordechai returned to the farmhouse. When he told Chaya what the Rabbi had said, she couldn't believe her ears.

"The Rabbi is bewitched," she cried. "What is he telling us to do? Look at my house. Look what he has made us do already . . . there are chickens wherever you look, clucking and squawking and dropping eggs and feathers all over the floor, the cow knocks over all the furniture and pulls the door off its hinges, my linen drawer has become a manger full of straw, and now he wants us to bring in the goat as well . . . and tie him to the end of our bed. It's too much!" She sat down at the table and wept salty tears into the dough she had been kneading.

"But you said yourself," said Mordechai, "he is an educated man, and so we should at least try it." So Chaya wiped her tears away and went to fetch the goat.

The next day, Chaya went with Mordechai to see the Rabbi. They sat at the table and Chaya spoke first.

"My husband has been to you before," she said, "and you have advised him and we have followed your advice. Yesterday you told us to bring in the goat, and we did it, and today we are both three-quarters of the way to our graves. It wasn't the fact that the goat ate every single thing it could reach, including a piece from my husband's nightshirt. After all, what do I own that's too precious for a goat to eat? Nothing, that's what. No, Rabbi, what finally drove us to seek your help is the stench. Have you ever slept within three feet of a goat? I thought my last hour had come. We have not slept a wink all night. Tell us, Rabbi, what do we do now?"

The Rabbi did not mutter, nor did he mumble. He did not fix his eyes on interesting spots anywhere in the room. Instead, he spoke straight to Mordechai and Chaya.

"Take the goat and the cow and the chickens out of your house. Return them to their own quarters. Then clean your house from top to bottom, and come and tell me how you feel."

Two days later, Mordechai and Chaya returned to the Rabbi's house.

"Oh, thank you, thank you, Rabbi," they said. "Our house is restored to us. It is clean and quiet and it doesn't smell of goat!"

"But what about Mordechai's mother? Do you not find it crowded?" said the Rabbi.

"Crowded?" said Mordechai. "It's like a palace."

"Paradise!" agreed Chaya. "I shall never complain about it ever again."

And she never did.'

Further reading

Adèle Geras has written many children's books as well as poetry and adult fiction. You can visit her website (http://www.adelegeras.com), where she encourages readers to e-mail her with their reactions to her stories. You might also enjoy the novel *Silent Snow Secret Snow* (Macmillan Children's Books, 2003), about a family Christmas.

Ramadan: Why Muslim Families Fast

by Kiran Ansari

> Kiran Ansari is an American Muslim. She describes herself as a writer, an editor and a 'mom'. She writes extensively on the Internet, including articles about Muslim issues and family advice.

Imran Ali, 7, leads the 5 pm family prayers in their Hickory Hills home as Eeba, 8, Ammar, 4, and his mother Aisha Ali follow.

Huma Murad's three daughters have been fasting at Ramadan since they were 7 years old – a choice they made to show their commitment to Islam and the holy month.

'Now that Fatimah, Amnah and Sarah are 17, 14 and 10, respectively, they don't find fasting difficult,' says Murad... And Murad says it was something they helped the girls learn to do over the years.

'We never forced our children, but they insisted on emulating us,' says Murad. 'At first, we just allowed them to keep a weekend "half-fast" where they could eat at lunch time. However, as the years passed by, fasting became habitual.

Ramadan, the ninth month of the Islamic calendar, is considered the holiest month in the year because it is the month in which God revealed the Qur'an or the Muslim's Holy Book, through Angel Gabriel to the Prophet Muhammad about 1,400 years ago.

During the month of Ramadan, Muslims fast from dawn to dusk to instill the virtues of patience and piety. They have a small meal, Suhur, before sunrise, then abstain from food and drink until Iftar, the meal at sunset.

With more than 7 million American and immigrant Muslims in the United States, Ramadan and Eid, the celebration that follows, are no longer foreign terms. Presidents and first ladies have hosted and attended Iftar parties. Hallmark now sells Eid (rhymes with reed) cards, retailers are beginning to sell decorations and some libraries ask the Muslim community to set up a Ramadan display with books and tapes to be checked out.

The month is to teach important lessons that go beyond refraining from food. At its heart, the holiday encourages the development of good qualities in both parents and children while teaching people how to refrain from negative habits.

Children are not required to fast until they reach puberty, but nine out of 10 Muslim children fast voluntarily.

'Even though my 10-year-old son, Abdul Rahman, really loves food, he fasted for the whole month last Ramadan,' says Rasha el-Khatib of Villa Park.

Parents know it is crucial for them to be their children's role models. 'The responsibility to set a good example lies on us,' says Huma. She continues: 'We can't leave it to pop stars and action heroes to be our children's ideals. Fasting teaches restraint from the lawful so that it becomes easier to refrain from the unlawful. It isn't just about staying hungry and thirsty. It's also about staying away from lying, backbiting and hurting others.'

It's easier for the children who attend private Islamic schools to observe Ramadan because the schools close the cafeteria for the month and the children are let out an hour earlier. This allows children and parents time to squeeze in a nap or prepare for Iftar.

Challenges and charity

Children attending secular schools face more challenges keeping their fast and finding a place for afternoon prayers.

Rasha el-Khatib's daughter, Rahaf Damar, 9, reads in the library during lunch time when she is fasting.

'In my children's public school in Des Plaines,' says Kishwar Rehman, 'the Muslim parents spoke to the teachers in advance and they, in turn, were very cooperative.

'The Muslim children were provided a room for prayer and they could stay back in class while the others went for lunch.

However, peer pressure can be tough. Seeing their friends eat may tempt some children to break their fast,' she says.

Fasting at public schools or at work does invite plenty of questions. 'My neighbor asked me why I keep my kids hungry all day. I explained that the kids are never forced to fast. This is what they want to do. They have a nutritious Suhur and a delicious Iftar to look forward to. Fasting instills a feeling of gratitude because when they feel the pangs of hunger, they get a sense of what the less fortunate have to deal with every day. Our children know that their hunger is just temporary,' says Rehman.

Generally, younger children begin with a half-fast on weekends. When they are older and want to fast voluntarily, parents encourage them to fast for the entire day, perhaps starting with only two fasts during the month. Children who commit to fasting are expected to fast the entire day, breaking their fast only if they fall ill.

Fasting begins with Suhur, the pre-dawn meal. 'I make sure that we all have a nutritious Suhur,' says Schaumburg mom Tazeen Hussain. 'Some families prefer a regular breakfast of cereal and eggs, but we prefer traditional foods like kebobs and parathas (hand-made fried bread). Along with the kids, I make sure I eat well, too.' . . .

Anticipation and Eid

Eid-ul-Fitr marks the end of Ramadan. Celebrated this year during the last week of November, Eid is a time for gratitude, rejoicing and sharing. Every household has its own unique way of marking the holiday, as well as the countdown to Eid.

On the first day of Ramadan, Dr Saima Azfar of Hoffman Estates makes a chain of 30 crescents out of construction paper and hangs it from the wall of her 5- and 6-year-olds' bedroom. Every day they pull down one crescent so that they know they are a day closer to Eid . . .

Often, Ramadan preparations start long before the holy month begins. Many parents spend time cooking and

A Muslim Eid celebration.

shopping to try and make family favorites such as egg rolls, kebobs and chutneys in advance and freeze them. This gives everyone more time to devote to worship and charity during Ramadan . . .

Eid day begins with families going for the Eid prayer held at various centers and banquet halls around the country. Before the prayer begins, every attendee contributes a minimum of $5 as 'Zakat-ul-Fitr', which loosely translates to mean obligatory charity after Ramadan. The money is distributed among the poor. 'We also try to make goody bags for the less fortunate kids so that they, too, have something to look forward to. In addition to candy and small toys, last year we included toothbrushes and school supplies,' says Hussain.

Students who attend Islamic schools get a few days off school and make up that time later. If Eid falls on a weekday, some parents return to work after prayers; others take the day off.

Families visit each other during the next couple of days . . .

Islamic organizations and local mosques often host Eid gatherings where people enjoy a variety of dishes from various Muslim countries . . .

'There are some dishes that have become associated with Ramadan,' says el-Khatib. Originally from Palestine, she feels that Iftar is incomplete without fattoosh (salad), juice made from dried apricots and katayef (dessert) . . .

Whether it's the 'Eidee' that excites the kids, the fancy new clothes that girls look forward to or the 'sheer korma' (dessert) that adults wait for, Eid is a holiday that serves to give children a reward – a pat on the back for a job well done.

Further reading

Kiran Ansari has a blog, mainly about bringing up her family, and her website http://www.kiranansari.com has links to more information about the Muslim faith.

Family Forum: Our Family Mealtimes Are Battlegrounds

Guardian readers' letters

Each Saturday, the *Guardian* newspaper has a 'Family' section which includes a discussion topic. One correspondent writes in with a problem, and readers respond with their solutions. Plenty of people had strong views on the topic of meals . . .

Different meals for everyone at mealtimes – vegi son, daughter won't eat pasta, dad picky – should I pander? Should I fight? If so, how? **SH**, *by e-mail*

For God's sake! Vegi son: cook vegetarian at least twice a week anyhow. You will all be healthier if you don't eat meat every day. Try to provide a vegi variation sometimes, i.e. chilli con carne without carne.

Daughter won't eat pasta: unless everyone else loves it, don't make it more than once a week. For that one day, tell her, tough! She can just eat the sauce and salad without the pasta. She will survive.

Dad picky: if this is your partner, your relationship is in serious trouble. You are in it together. Talk to him. Why would you make things he really hates? Balance this idea with, what kind of adult is 'picky', for God's sake? It's not hard to imagine where your daughter is learning her 'picky' food neurosis.

If they can't cook, teach them, one meal at a time, one person at a time. Smile when the food is served. Eat it. **DA**, *by e-mail*

I was 14 when I informed my mother that I was turning vegetarian. Her response was: 'That's great but you'll have to cook for yourself.' **ES**, *by e-mail*

My mum catered for the lowest common denominator – my (picky) dad. Mealtimes were not the most varied occasions. I didn't find out what broccoli tasted like until my housemate cooked it at university. It was torture for my mum who loves all food (except green peppers and aubergines). I think it would be a real mistake to repeat that in your house . . .

Those who don't like the food may help themselves to a healthy meal of bread, cheese and fruit. Tell your husband his pickiness is a bad example; say it's become wearying for you so you'll now ignore it.

Tell your son vegetarian food can be more work, but you'll accommodate him as much as you can. Ask him to research a few delicious meat-free dishes for dinner. Serve pasta just occasionally. If spaghetti bolognese, offer your daughter leftover spuds/rice instead of pasta; if she's not too little, she could cook this herself. **MW**, *by e-mail*

Provide one meal with various elements, and people can leave what they choose not to eat. If they're hungry again later, do what our parents and grandparents (and no doubt theirs as well) did, and say, 'There's plenty of bread in the bread bin and fruit in the fruitbowl.' **DD**, *on the talkboard*

My mother-in-law pandered to her children by having a large range of food on the table at each mealtime – still does in fact when we visit. The result is that my husband and sister-in-law are incredibly fussy eaters still in their 30s, and the only reason my brother-in-law isn't is that his wife won't let him. **TS**, *on the talkboard*

If dad is picky then you are acting like his mum. Sort out the relationship as it sounds like you have one extra child. **GY**, *on the talkboard*

The danger with letting the dad sort himself out is that, if like my husband, he will live on sandwiches and shop-made pies, thereby damaging his own health and setting a lousy example! **DD**, *on the talkboard*

My kids all get the same meals, but do tend to enter into negotiations over what they can swap between each other. This usually involves the five-year-old exchanging his peas for the two-year-old's potatoes. **BV**, *on the talkboard*

Family Forum: Our Family Mealtimes Are Battlegrounds

I was a picky eater as a child. I remember traumatic mealtimes with parents sat either side of me forcing me to eat. I remember how stressed they used to get. I was anorexic in my teens and though I don't blame them wholly for this, I'm sure that I learned a lesson very early on that I could use food (or rather refusal of it) as a way of getting at them.

I promised myself that I would make sure my son had no hangups and so if he does not eat what I give him, he goes hungry. No hassle, no pleading – the plate is taken away and he gets nothing. **TI**, *on the talkboard*

We don't bother with family meals, just cook what we want when we're hungry. **BA**, *on the talkboard*

Picky eaters are a pet hate of mine, and in my experience are created by overindulgent parents. It may seem like you're being a loving and dutiful mother by trying to make your little darlings happy, but you're just setting them up to be the objects of mockery by more normal people in adulthood. **CI**, *on the talkboard*

Family meals.

(www.CartoonStock.com)

Home cafeteria. (www.CartoonStock.com)

My ex's mother used to cook him *three* different meals every night so he could decide what he wanted. Funny, he has never married... **VW**, *on the talkboard*

Further reading

The 'Family' section in the Saturday *Guardian* is full of interest for all members of the family, and often includes articles about life with teenagers.

A Gentleman's Agreement
by Elizabeth Jolley

> A poor Australian family stick together through hard times and find happiness through a clever idea . . .

In the home science lesson I had to unpick my darts as Mrs Kay said they were all wrong and then I scorched the collar of my dress because I had the iron too hot. And then the sewing machine needle broke and there wasn't a spare and Mrs Kay got really wild and Peril Page cut all the notches off her pattern by mistake and that finished everything.

'I'm not ever going back to that school,' I said to Mother in the evening. 'I'm finished with that place!' So that was my brother and me both leaving school before we should have and my brother kept leaving jobs too, one job after another, sometimes not even staying long enough in one place to wait for his pay.

But Mother was worrying about what to get for my brother's tea.

'What about a bit of lamb's fry and bacon,' I said. She brightened up then and, as she was leaving to go up the terrace for her shopping, she said, 'You can come with me tomorrow then and we'll get through the work quicker.' She didn't seem to mind at all that I had left school.

Mother cleaned in a large block of luxury apartments. She had keys to the flats and she came and went as she pleased and as her work demanded. It was while she was working there that she had the idea of letting the people from down our street taste the pleasures rich people took for granted in their way of living. While these people were away to their offices or on business trips she let our poor neighbours in. We had wedding receptions and parties in the penthouse and the old folk came in to soak their feet and wash their clothes while Mother was doing the cleaning. As she said, she gave a lot of pleasure to people without doing anybody any harm, though it was often a terrible rush for her. She could never refuse anybody anything and, because of this, always had more work than she could manage and more people to be kind to than her time really allowed.

Sometimes at the weekends I went with Mother to look at Grandpa's valley. It was quite a long bus ride. We had to get off at the twenty-nine-mile peg, cross the Medulla brook and walk up a country road with scrub[1] on either side till we came to some cleared acres of pasture which was the beginning of her father's land. She struggled through the wire fence hating the mud. She wept out loud because the old man hung on to his land and all his money was buried, as she put it, in the sodden meadows of cape weed and stuck fast in the outcrops of granite higher up where all the topsoil had washed away. She couldn't sell the land because Grandpa was still alive in a Home for the Aged, and he wanted to keep the farm though he couldn't do anything with it. Even sheep died there. They either starved or got drowned depending on the time of the year. It was either drought there or flood. The weatherboard house was so neglected it was falling apart, the tenants were feckless, and if a calf was born there it couldn't get up, that was the kind of place it was. When we went to see Grandpa he wanted to know about the farm and Mother tried to think of things to please him. She didn't say the fence posts were crumbling away and that the castor oil plants had taken over the yard so you couldn't get through to the barn.

There was an old apricot tree in the middle of the meadow, it was as big as a house and a terrible burden to us to get the fruit at just the right time. Mother liked to take some to the hospital so that Grandpa could keep up his pride and self-respect a bit.

In the full heat of the day I had to pick with an apron tied round me, it had deep pockets for the fruit. I grabbed at the green fruit when I thought Mother wasn't looking and pulled off whole branches so it wouldn't be there to be picked later.

---

[1] **scrub**   large wild area covered with small trees; the Australian Bush

'Don't take that branch!' Mother screamed from the ground. 'Them's not ready yet. We'll have to come back tomorrow for them.'

I lost my temper and pulled off the apron full of fruit and hurled it down but it stuck on a branch and hung there quite out of reach either from up the tree where I was or from the ground.

'Wait! Just you wait till I get a holt of you!' Mother pranced round the tree and I didn't come down till we had missed our bus and it was getting dark and all the dogs in the little township barked as if they were insane, the way dogs do in the country, as we walked through trying to get a lift home.

One Sunday in the winter it was very cold but Mother thought we should go all the same. We passed some sheep huddled in a natural fold of furze and withered grass all frost sparkling in the morning.

'Quick!' Mother said. 'We'll grab a sheep and take a bit of wool back to Grandpa.'

'But they're not our sheep,' I said.

'Never mind!' And she was in among the sheep before I could stop her. The noise was terrible but she managed to grab a bit of wool.

'It's terrible dirty and shabby,' she complained, pulling at the shreds with her cold fingers. 'I don't think I've ever seen such miserable wool.'

All that evening she was busy with the wool, she did make me laugh.

'How will modom have her hair done?' She put the wool on the kitchen table and kept walking all round it talking to it. She tried to wash it and comb it but it still looked awful so she put it round one of my curlers for the night.

'I'm really ashamed of the wool,' Mother said next morning.

'But it isn't ours,' I said.

'I know but I'm ashamed all the same,' she said. So when we were in the penthouse at South Heights she cut a tiny piece off the bathroom mat. It was so soft and silky. And later we went to visit Grandpa. He was sitting with his poor paralysed legs under his tartan rug.

'Here's a bit of the wool clip Dad,' Mother said, bending over to kiss him. His whole face lit up.

'That's nice of you to bring it, really nice.' His old fingers stroked the little piece of nylon carpet.

'It's very good, deep and soft.' He smiled at Mother.

'They do wonderful things with sheep these days Dad,' she said.

'They do indeed,' he said, and all the time he was feeling the bit of carpet.

'Are you pleased Dad?' Mother asked him anxiously. 'You are pleased aren't you?'

'Oh yes I am,' he assured her.

I thought I saw a moment of disappointment in his eyes, but the eyes of old people often look full of tears.

On the way home I tripped on the steps.

'Ugh! I felt your bones!' Really Mother was so thin it hurt to fall against her.

'Well what d'you expect me to be, a boneless wonder?'

Really Mother had such a hard life and we lived in such a cramped and squalid place. She longed for better things and she needed a good rest. I wished more than anything the old man would agree to selling his land. Because he wouldn't sell I found myself wishing he would die and whoever really wants to wish someone to die! It was only that it would sort things out a bit for us.

In the supermarket Mother thought and thought what she could get for my brother for his tea. In the end all she could come up with was fish fingers and a packet of jelly beans.

'You know I never eat fish! And I haven't eaten sweets in years.' My brother looked so tall in the kitchen. He lit a cigarette and slammed out and Mother was too tired and too upset to eat her own tea.

Grandpa was an old man and though his death was expected it was unexpected really and it was a shock to Mother to find she suddenly had eighty-seven acres to sell. And there was the house too. She had a terrible lot to do as she decided to sell the property herself and, at the same time, she did not want to let down the people at South Heights. There was a man interested to buy the land, Mother had kept him up her sleeve for years, ever since he had stopped once by the bottom paddock to ask if it was for sale. At the time Mother would have given her right arm to be able to sell it and she promised he should have first refusal if it ever came on the market.

We all three, Mother and myself and my brother, went out at the weekend to tidy things up. We lost my brother and then we suddenly saw him running and running and shouting, his voice lifting up in the wind as he raced up the slope of the valley.

'I do believe he's laughing! He's happy!' Mother just stared at him and she looked so happy too.

I don't think I ever saw the country look so lovely before.

The tenant was standing by the shed. The big tractor had crawled to the doorway like a sick animal and had stopped there, but in no time my brother had it going.

It seemed there was nothing my brother couldn't do. Suddenly after doing nothing in his life he was driving the tractor and making fire breaks, he started to paint the sheds and he told Mother what fencing posts and wire to order. All these things had to be done before the sale could go through. We all had a wonderful time in the country. I kept wishing we could live in the house, all at once it seemed lovely there at the top of the sunlit meadow. But I knew that however many acres you have, they aren't any use unless you have money too. I think we were all thinking this but no one said anything though Mother kept looking at my brother and the change in him.

There was no problem about the price of the land, this man, he was a doctor, really wanted it and Mother really needed the money.

'You might as well come with me,' Mother said to me on the day of the sale. 'You can learn how business is done.' So we sat in this lawyer's comfortable room and he read out from various papers and the doctor signed things and Mother signed. Suddenly she said to them, 'You know my father really loved his farm but he only managed to have it late in life and then he was never able to live there because of his illness.' The two men looked at her.

'I'm sure you will understand,' she said to the doctor, 'with your own great love of the land, my father's love for his valley. I feel if I could live there just to plant one crop and stay while it matures, my father would rest easier in his grave.'

'Well I don't see why not.' The doctor was really a kind man. The lawyer began to protest, he seemed quite angry.

'It's not in the agreement,' he began to say. But the doctor silenced him, he got up and came round to Mother's side of the table.

'I think you should live there and plant your one crop and stay while it matures,' he said to her. 'It's a gentleman's agreement,' he said.

'That's the best sort.' Mother smiled up at him and they shook hands.

'I wish your crop well,' the doctor said, still shaking her hand. The doctor made the lawyer write out a special clause which they all signed. And then we left, everyone satisfied. Mother had never had so much money and the doctor had the valley at last but it was the gentleman's agreement which was the best part.

My brother was impatient to get on with improvements.

'There's no rush,' Mother said.

'Well one crop isn't very long,' he said.

'It's long enough,' she said.

So we moved out to the valley and the little weatherboard cottage seemed to come to life very quickly with the pretty things we chose for the rooms.

'It's nice whichever way you look out from these little windows,' Mother was saying and just then her crop arrived. The carter set down the boxes along the edge of the verandah and, when he had gone, my brother began to unfasten the hessian[2] coverings. Inside were hundreds of seedlings in little plastic containers.

'What are they?' he asked.

'Our crop,' Mother said.

'Yes I know, but what is the crop? What are these?'

'Them,' said Mother, she seemed unconcerned, 'oh they're a jarrah[3] forest,' she said.

'But that will take years and years to mature,' he said.

'I know,' Mother said. 'We'll start planting tomorrow. We'll pick the best places and clear and plant as we go along.'

'But what about the doctor?' I said, somehow I could picture him pale and patient by his car out on the lonely road which went through his valley. I seemed to see him looking with longing at his paddocks and his meadows and at his slopes of scrub and bush.

'Well he can come on his land whenever he wants to and have a look at us,' Mother said. 'There's nothing in the gentleman's agreement to say he can't.'

Further reading

There are several other family stories in Elizabeth Jolley's collection, *Fellow Passengers* (Penguin Books Australia Ltd, 1997). You might also enjoy her novel *Cabin Fever* (HarperPerennial, 1992), about an unmarried mother.

---

[2]**hessian** sacking material
[3]**jarrah** an Australian hardwood tree

My Parents
by Adrian Mitchell

> Adrian Mitchell is probably most famous for the poetry he wrote during the 1960s, including *I Like That Stuff*, familiar from many anthologies, and *To Whom It May Concern*, about the Vietnam war, which he read in Trafalgar Square in 1964. His writing is passionate, humorous, and always surprising. The text that follows comes from an anthology, *Worlds: Seven Modern Poets* (Penguin Books Ltd, 1986).

My father died the other day and I would like to write about him. Because I think of them together, this means also writing about my mother, who died several years ago.

About a thousand people called her Kay, most of them people she helped at some time, for she was what chintzy[1] villains call a 'dogooder' Nobody ever called her that to her face or in my family's hearing; if they had, she'd have felt sorry for them. Both her brothers were killed in the First World War. She divided her life between loving her family, bullying or laughing innumerable committees into action rather than talk, giving, plotting happiness for other people, and keeping up an exuberant correspondence with several hundred friends.

She was not afraid of anyone. She was right. A Fabian[2] near-pacifist,[3] she encouraged me to argue, assuming right-wing positions sometimes so that I was forced to fight and win the discussion.

She tried to hoist the whole world on her shoulders. After each of her first two cancer operations, on her breasts, she seemed to clench her fists and double the energy with which she gave. She wasn't interested in unshared pleasure.

---

[1]**chintzy** stingy, miserly
[2]**Fabian** politically left-wing, believing that the community as a whole has a responsibility to its individual members, particularly the weaker ones
[3]**near-pacifist** someone opposed to war in most circumstances

After the second operation she answered the door one day to a poor woman whom she didn't know. The woman asked where 'the wise woman' lived. My mother knew whom she meant – a rich clairvoyant who lived down the road. Not trusting that particular witch, my mother asked what was wrong. The poor woman's doctor had told her that she must have a breast removed, and she was very scared. My mother said, but there's nothing to that, look – and she took out the two rolled socks which she kept in her empty brassiere and threw them up into the sunlight and then caught them again. So the poor woman came in, drank tea, talked, forgot many fears, and went away knowing that she had seen the wise woman.

People called my father Jock. Face tanned from working in his garden, he survived the trenches of the First World War. He spoke very little. When he talked it was either very funny or very important. He only spoke to me about his war twice, and then briefly. In my teens I wrote a short, Owen-influenced[4] poem about the war. My father read it, then told me of a friend who, during the lull between bombardments, fell to all fours and howled like an animal and was never cured.

Usually he avoided company. There was something in other people which frightened him. He was right. At the seaside he would sit on the farthest-out rock and fish peacefully. When visitors called at our house he would generally disappear into his jungle of raspberry canes and lurk.

Maybe there were twenty or thirty people in the world whose company he really enjoyed. They were lucky; he was a lovely man. Like Edward Lear,[5] he was most at his ease with children, who instantly read, in the lines radiating from the corners of his eyes, that this was a man who understood their games and jokes.

After my mother's death, he was a desolated man. But when he remarried, very happily, light came back into his face

---

[4]**Owen-influenced**   in the style of Wilfred Owen, a World War I poet
[5]**Edward Lear**   a humorous poet, famous for his limericks and nonsense verse

and he learned to smile again. He was short and lean and had fantastic sprouting Scottish eyebrows. He was a research chemist, but that didn't mean he only took an interest and pride in my elder brother's scientific work. He let me see how glad he was that I wrote, and I still remember the stories he used to write for me and my brother.

A year or so before he died he was in London for the day. My father sometimes voted Tory, sometimes Liberal, but when he began to talk about Vietnam that day, his face became first red and then white with anger about the cruelty and stupidity of the war. I seldom saw him angry and never so angry as at that moment, a man of seventy, not much interested in politics, all the grief of 1914–18 marching back into his mind.

People sometimes talk as if the ideological[6] conflicts between generations have to be fought out bloodily, as if it is inevitable that children should grow to hate their parents. I don't believe this. Our family was lucky: my brother and I were always free to choose for ourselves – knowing that, however odd our decisions, we were trusted and loved. We all loved one another and this love was never shadowed.

Further reading

Adrian Mitchell is a prolific poet, writing for children as well as adults. A recent collection, *Daft as a Doughnut* (Orchard Books, 2004), demonstrates his special mixture of humour and challenge. He has written many plays, plus TV and radio scripts. You can find out more about him from his website, http://www.rippingyarns.co.uk/adrian, and from http://www.poetryarchive.org, where you can listen to an interview with him and recordings of his poetry.

---

[6]**ideological**   concerned with ideas

Forging a Family
by Sue Palmer

> This extract comes from *Toxic Childhood: How the Modern World Is Damaging Our Children and What We Can Do about It* (Orion, 2007). Sue Palmer is a journalist and education consultant who cares passionately about family life. But it can be difficult to keep it going in today's frantic world . . .

In order to forge a viable family, the 'adults in charge' have to be physically present for a reasonable amount of time every week. This means sorting out their work–life balance so that, even if they work full-time, they still spend plenty of time at home. A recent snippet of Internet wisdom put the case rather well: 'If you died tomorrow, the company that employs you would fill your place within a week or so; your family would miss you for ever.' Indeed, in many cases they're missing you already, and toxic childhood is the result.

All the experts I've met and read on the subject of family welfare and social cohesion[1] condemn the long-hours culture and commend flexible working practices. Families don't flourish unless their members spend time together, so it really is time that governments, businesses and individual human beings got their act together on this one – as the journalist Richard Reeves puts it, if our culture is to have a future we need to create family-friendly economies, not economy-friendly families.

When families don't spend enough time in each other's company, special events such as Christmas, special celebrations or holidays are often a terrible disappointment. In a 2005 UK survey, 75 per cent of parents said they found family holidays stressful, even though they were supposed to be a precious opportunity to spend more 'quality time' with their children.

---

[1] **cohesion**   sticking together

As social psychologist Pat Spungin says, if parents and children don't spend time together on a regular basis, 'the pressure on everyone to be having a perfect time and the feeling this is a one-off chance can permeate every aspect of the holiday to increase overall stress levels'.

Given that time is available, much of the experts' advice for creating strong families applies to everyone involved, whether they're biologically related or not. For instance, families need to develop their identity as a group, which means shared interests and activities. Adults also need time to bond with children one-to-one – while of course avoiding any suggestion of favouritism between siblings and/or step-siblings.

This one-to-one time doesn't have to be spent doing anything special – indeed, one of the most important parental tasks is to pass on simple life skills to the next generation, just by involving them in day-to-day tasks... There's no rush to achieve, no competition, no prizes – it's just a question of taking your time over the years, gradually initiating your child into adult skills. Involving children in a hobby, sport or other interest can also be fulfilling for both generations. Whether it's sewing or cinema-going, fishing or supporting a football team, parents who pass on their passions to their children always have a point of communication, even during the difficult years of adolescence.

There's another element of balance here. Spending time with children doesn't mean having to be with them interminably – especially as the children grow older, and their social circle widens. But when adults *are* in the bosom of the family, we should be free to engage with children rather than wishing them out of the way. That means switching off mobile phones, ignoring the e-mail, and concentrating on the chosen family activity, or just chatting with and listening to the children. It's shifting from the rapid pace of everyday life to 'slow time', and it's not only good for your family, it's good for your health.

To ensure time spent together is as pleasant an experience as possible, families need carefully formulated policies on issues like discipline, mealtime behaviour, bedtimes, and so on.

American researchers Betty Hart and Todd Risley, who analysed 42 US families over two and a half years, concluded that 'what made a family normal was its stable and predictable ways of interacting'. Very young children obviously should have little input into family policies – adults are in charge because they know what's good for them – but as children grow older and wiser, there's room for increased negotiation. At all stages, adults have to agree on a reasonable policy, then keep up a united front (trying never to row in front of the children) and act as role models for the sorts of behaviour they want to see.

For adults who are not biologically related to children in their family, one frequently given piece of advice is to acknowledge the fact that you're not a blood relation. The inevitable stepchild's cry of 'You're not my mum/dad!' can be countered immediately with 'You're right. I could never even try to replace your mum/dad. But I'm the adult in charge at the moment, so what I say goes.' Experts generally agree that biological parents should take the lead in discipline, making it clear that other 'adults in charge' are their trusted lieutenants.

Now that many children divide their time between two family homes, it helps if basic rules for behaviour, bedtime and so on are consistent; if they aren't, acceptable boundaries in your own home must be very clearly drawn. Schedules and arrangements for visits are important to children, so it helps if they're easily manageable – if they're not, it behoves adults to put themselves out so children are not let down.

That is what forging a family is all about: adults putting themselves out so children's developmental needs are met. In the revolutionary whirlwind of the last twenty-five years, the focus has been firmly on the needs of adults – the changes in their roles and the resultant dramas in their relationships. The Archbishop of Canterbury summed up our current problems in a speech in 2005: 'Children are so caught up in the energy of adult dramas that they do not have the space . . . in which to be securely children ... We have to accept that growing up is about taking on the task of forming other human lives.'

The family – love it or hate it – is where the grown-up generation forms the generation to come. It's where parents, and other adults-in-charge, develop children's sense of self, security and self-esteem, their ability to get along with other people, their knowledge about life and life skills, and an inner code of conduct to guide and protect them when we're no longer around. So far the human race hasn't come up with any better way of passing on these essential elements of our culture. The family is where, in the words of the old adage, we give our children 'roots to grow and wings to fly'.

Further reading

There has been a great flood of advice recently about creating happy families – you may have seen TV programmes such as *Little Angels*, which exists in book form as well (BBC Active, 2005). Another helpful and humorous book, told in comic-strip format and suitable for parents and their children to read together, is *How to Talk So Kids Will Listen and Listen So Kids Will Talk* (Piccadilly Press Ltd, 2001).

A Christmas Carol

by Charles Dickens

> *A Christmas Carol* is a well-known classic which tells the story of Ebenezer Scrooge, a miser who believes that the spirit of Christmas is all 'humbug'. On Christmas Eve he is visited by three ghosts, of Christmas Past, Christmas Present and Christmas Future, who teach him the error of his ways. Here he is magically transported by the Ghost of Christmas Present to visit the family of his poor but uncomplaining clerk, Bob Cratchit, as they eat their dinner on Christmas Day. With a large family to feed and a sick son, Tiny Tim, Bob's meagre salary doesn't stretch very far. But nothing can dampen the Cratchits' spirits . . .

Then up rose Mrs Cratchit, Cratchit's wife, dressed out but poorly in a twice-turned[1] gown, but brave in ribbons, which are cheap and make a goodly show for sixpence; and she laid the cloth, assisted by Belinda Cratchit, second of her daughters, also brave in ribbons; while Master Peter Cratchit plunged a fork into the saucepan of potatoes, and getting the corners of his monstrous shirt collar (Bob's private property, conferred upon his son and heir in honour of the day) into his mouth, rejoiced to find himself so gallantly attired, and yearned to show his linen in the fashionable Parks. And now two smaller Cratchits, boy and girl, came tearing in, screaming that outside the baker's they had smelt the goose, and known it for their own; and basking in luxurious thoughts of sage-and-onion, these young Cratchits danced about the table, and exalted Master Peter Cratchit to the skies, while he (not proud, although his collars nearly choked him) blew the fire, until the slow potatoes bubbling up, knocked loudly at the saucepan-lid to be let out and peeled.

---

[1] **twice-turned** turned inside-out to make it look newer

'What has ever got your precious father then?' said Mrs Cratchit. 'And your brother, Tiny Tim! And Martha warn't as late last Christmas Day by half-an-hour!'

'Here's Martha, mother!' said a girl, appearing as she spoke.

'Here's Martha, mother!' cried the two young Cratchits. 'Hurrah! There's *such* a goose, Martha!'

'Why, bless your heart alive, my dear, how late you are!' said Mrs Cratchit, kissing her a dozen times, and taking off her shawl and bonnet for her with officious zeal.

'We'd a deal of work to finish up last night,' replied the girl, 'and had to clear away this morning, mother!'

'Well! Never mind so long as you are come,' said Mrs Cratchit. 'Sit ye down before the fire, my dear, and have a warm, Lord bless ye!'

'No, no! There's father coming,' cried the two young Cratchits, who were everywhere at once. 'Hide, Martha, hide!'

So Martha hid herself, and in came little Bob, the father, with at least three feet of comforter[2] exclusive of the fringe, hanging down before him; and his threadbare clothes darned up and brushed, to look seasonable; and Tiny Tim upon his shoulder. Alas for Tiny Tim, he bore a little crutch, and had his limbs supported by an iron frame!

'Why, where's our Martha?' cried Bob Cratchit, looking round.

'Not coming,' said Mrs Cratchit.

'Not coming!' said Bob, with a sudden declension in his high spirits; for he had been Tim's blood horse[3] all the way from church, and had come home rampant. 'Not coming upon Christmas Day!'

Martha didn't like to see him disappointed, if it were only in joke; so she came out prematurely from behind the closet door, and ran into his arms, while the two young Cratchits hustled Tiny Tim, and bore him off into the wash-house, that he might hear the pudding singing in the copper.[4]

---

[2]**comforter** scarf
[3]**blood horse** thoroughbred horse
[4]**copper** a pot made of copper for boiling water

'And how did little Tim behave?' asked Mrs Cratchit, when she had rallied[5] Bob on his credulity,[6] and Bob had hugged his daughter to his heart's content.

'As good as gold,' said Bob, 'and better. Somehow he gets thoughtful, sitting by himself so much, and thinks the strangest things you ever heard. He told me, coming home, that he hoped the people saw him in the church, because he was a cripple, and it might be pleasant to them to remember upon Christmas Day, who made lame beggars walk and blind men see.'

Bob's voice was tremulous when he told them this, and trembled more when he said that Tiny Tim was growing strong and hearty.

His active little crutch was heard upon the floor, and back came Tiny Tim before another word was spoken, escorted by his brother and sister to his stool before the fire; and while Bob, turning up his cuffs – as if, poor fellow, they were capable of being made more shabby – compounded some hot mixture in a jug with gin and lemons, and stirred it round and round and put it on the hob to simmer; Master Peter and the two ubiquitous[7] young Cratchits went to fetch the goose, with which they soon returned in high procession.

Such a bustle ensued that you might have thought a goose the rarest of all birds; a feathered phenomenon, to which a black swan was a matter of course – and in truth it was something very like it in that house. Mrs Cratchit made the gravy (ready beforehand in a little saucepan) hissing hot; Master Peter mashed the potatoes with incredible vigour; Miss Belinda sweetened up the apple-sauce; Martha dusted the hot plates; Bob took Tiny Tim beside him in a tiny corner at the table; the two young Cratchits set chairs for everybody, not forgetting themselves, and mounting guard upon their posts, crammed

---

[5]**rallied**   teased
[6]**credulity**   willingness to believe too easily
[7]**ubiquitous**   seeming to be everywhere at once

God bless us every one!

spoons into their mouths, lest they should shriek for goose before their turn came to be helped. At last the dishes were set on, and grace was said. It was succeeded by a breathless pause, as Mrs Cratchit, looking slowly all along the carving-knife, prepared to plunge it in the breast; but when she did, and when the long-expected gush of stuffing issued forth, one murmur of delight arose all round the board, and even Tiny Tim, excited by the two young Cratchits, beat on the table with the handle of his knife, and feebly cried Hurrah!

There never was such a goose. Bob said he didn't believe there ever was such a goose cooked. Its tenderness and flavour, size and cheapness, were the themes of universal admiration. Eked out by the apple-sauce and mashed potatoes, it was a sufficient dinner for the whole family; indeed, as Mrs Cratchit said with great delight (surveying one small atom of a bone upon the dish), they hadn't ate it all at last! Yet every one had had enough, and the youngest Cratchits in particular, were steeped in sage and onion to the eyebrows! But now, the plates being changed by Miss Belinda, Mrs Cratchit left the room alone – too nervous to bear witnesses – to take the pudding up and bring it in.

Suppose it should not be done enough! Suppose it should break in turning out! Suppose somebody should have got over the wall of the back-yard, and stolen it, while they were merry with the goose – a supposition at which the two young Cratchits became livid! All sorts of horrors were supposed.

Halloa! A great deal of steam! The pudding was out of the copper. A smell like a washing-day! That was the cloth. A smell like an eating-house and a pastry-cook's next door to each other, with a laundress's next door to that! That was the pudding! In half a minute Mrs Cratchit entered – flushed, but smiling proudly – with the pudding, like a speckled cannon-ball, so hard and firm, blazing in half of half-a-quartern of ignited brandy, and bedight[8] with Christmas holly stuck into the top.

Oh, a wonderful pudding! Bob Cratchit said, and calmly too, that he regarded it as the greatest success achieved by Mrs Cratchit since their marriage. Mrs Cratchit said that now the weight was off her mind, she would confess she had had her doubts about the quantity of flour. Everybody had something to say about it, but nobody said or thought it was at all a small pudding for a large family. It would have been flat heresy[9] to do so. Any Cratchit would have blushed to hint at such a thing.

At last the dinner was all done, the cloth was cleared, the hearth swept, and the fire made up. The compound in the jug being tasted, and considered perfect, apples and oranges were put upon the table, and a shovel-full of chestnuts on the fire. Then all the Cratchit family drew round the hearth, in what

---

[8]**bedight**   decorated
[9]**heresy**   unacceptable opinion

Bob Cratchit called a circle, meaning half a one; and at Bob Cratchit's elbow stood the family display of glass. Two tumblers, and a custard-cup without a handle.

These held the hot stuff from the jug, however, as well as golden goblets would have done; and Bob served it out with beaming looks, while the chestnuts on the fire sputtered and cracked noisily. Then Bob proposed:

'A merry Christmas to us all, my dears. God bless us!'

Which all the family re-echoed.

'God bless us every one!' said Tiny Tim, the last of all.

Further reading

Although they were written over a hundred years ago, Dickens' novels are still best-sellers. Try *Oliver Twist* (Penguin Classics, 2003), *David Copperfield* (Oxford Paperbacks, 1999) or *Great Expectations* (Longman, 2004), all of which have been made into films and TV series, and which include unforgettable characters like the pickpocket Fagin, the charming villain Steerforth, or the eccentric Miss Havisham.

The Trouble Was Meals
by Elizabeth Bennett

> Like *A Christmas Carol*, this poem describes a family meal with some entertaining characters, but it is very different in tone. It comes from *When I Am an Old Woman I Shall Wear Purple* (Papier-Mâché Press, 2007), a collection of writings about the problems and pleasures of being old.

Dad was the head of the family, for sure.
When he got us all together
it meant either a baby was on the way
or we were moving. So when the question was put,
How would it be if Grandma came to live with us?
I thought, no big deal.
I was glad we weren't moving.

I found a picture of Grandma,
a young dancer in a dress, sequins and feathers.
She had me tape it onto the mirror
over the dresser where she kept Grandpa's remains,
his gold cuff links, glass eye.

It was all right,
Grandma the dancer in residence,
all right for me, hard for Mother.
Dad would come home, pour a glass of Old Crow bourbon,
one for Mother, drink them both.

The trouble was meals.
Dad was used to holding forth
and the first night, halfway through chicken cacciatore
Grandma turned and said, 'Rest your gums, dear.'
She called everyone dear, all of us, the mailman,

even the exterminator.¹
She took to humming in a loud voice
and dropping her knife and fork on the floor.
One night she shouted, 'Leftovers, leftovers,
where's the original?' and shoved her plate
on the floor. Baby threw his bottle
on top of the broken china. The plate crash
became a regular occurrence.

Fridays at school our teacher read us poetry,
'Poitry,' she called it. One went,
'Old age is a flight of small cheeping birds . . . '
I didn't like poetry. What I liked was shop.²
I made a wooden bowl, sanded the rim smooth,
carved my initials on the bottom.
I brought it home to Grandma
and we served her dinner in it every night.
She still shoved it on the floor
but nothing broke.

When I was at the orthodontist's one afternoon,
Grandma took a nap and never woke up.
We cleaned out her room. I helped Mother.
She was in a mood to throw everything out,
flannel sheets that smelled of urine, everything.
She only kept the picture. That night after dinner
I found the bowl in the trash.
Dad said, we won't need *that* anymore,
but I washed and dried it
and put it on the shelf next to Old Crow
so I could find it when Mother got old.

---

¹**exterminator**   person who gets rid of rats or mice
²**shop**   carpentry class

Further reading

When I Am an Old Woman I Shall Wear Purple is the first line of a famous poem, *Warning*, by Jenny Joseph. It describes all the outrageous things the writer plans to do in later life, which include wearing purple! There are other poems about grandparents by Berlie Doherty in her collection *Walking on Air* (Hodder Children's Books, 1999).

Activities

My House and *An Overcrowded House*

Before you read

1 Make a spider diagram by writing 'My house' in the middle of a blank page and then jotting down all the words that you associate with that phrase. Join the words to the centre to make a web. For instance, is your house overcrowded, quiet, noisy, quarrelsome, happy . . . ? Compare your word web with a partner's.

What's it about?

Read the poem and the story and answer questions 2 and 3 by yourself. Then compare your answers with a partner's.

2 In the poem, what is the house built out of? What do you think the poet means when she says she doesn't need sand and water?

3 In *An Overcrowded House*, why did the Rabbi's strange advice work so well? What is the moral of the story?

Thinking about the text

4 Which of the following adjectives best describe the mood of *My House* for you? Choose three and explain your choice, quoting examples from the poem. Are there any other adjectives you might use to describe it?

   simple   moving   direct   loving   childlike   joyous

   Then think of six adjectives to describe *An Overcrowded House*. Ask a classmate to choose three and give reasons for their choices.

5 Why do you think these two pieces have been put together? What do they have in common? Write two paragraphs comparing them. Pick out words and phrases from the texts to support your ideas. Think about:
   - the mood of both pieces
   - the relationships between the people
   - the atmosphere in the houses.

6 Use the library or Internet to research *either* the Jewish festival of the Passover (find out about *Hagadah* and *Seder*) *or* family life in Senegal. Prepare a short talk on it for the rest of the class.

Ramadan: Why Muslim Families Fast and *Family Forum: Our Family Mealtimes Are Battlegrounds*

Before you read

1 What are your family mealtimes like? Times to dread, or sources of pleasure? Do you eat together? Do you all eat the same food? Do you argue about it? Compare notes in a small group.

2 Do you know how many different faiths are represented in your school? Are there special arrangements made – for example, to allow time off for holy days, or to follow special diets? Working in a small group, make a chart that could be used to explain the school's arrangements to a visitor.

What's it about?

Read the two texts and answer questions 3 and 4 by yourself. Then compare your answers with a partner's.

3 Read the following statements and decide, based on the information in the texts, whether they are facts or opinions.
- Most Muslim children join their parents fasting at Ramadan.
- It's crucial for parents to be role models for their children.
- Most men live on sandwiches and shop-made pies.
- Seeing their friends eating tempts children to break their fast.
- Some people cook different meals for everyone at mealtimes.
- Students at Islamic schools often get time off during Ramadan.
- If you pander to your children they'll be picky eaters.

4 In two paragraphs, sum up how the parents in each text try to influence their children's eating habits, and why.

Thinking about the text

5 Using ideas from the texts, hold a debate in your class or small group on the following topic: 'Parents make more important role models than pop stars or action heroes.'

6 Plan an interview with someone in your school or class who is willing to talk about their faith and its traditions. You could ask about:
- special celebrations
- religious services
- rules about dress
- traditional food.

A Gentleman's Agreement

Before you read

1 What do you understand by the phrase of the title, 'a gentleman's agreement'? Discuss your ideas with a partner.

What's it about?

Discuss questions 2 and 3 with a partner, and make brief notes together to share with the rest of the class or group.

2 How did Mother persuade the doctor to let her plant one crop? Why do you think he agreed to her suggestion?

3 What do you think the narrator feels about her mother? Collect evidence from the text to justify your opinions.

Thinking about the text

4 What does the family like and dislike about Grandfather's valley? What do you think is the clinching thing that makes them want to keep it? Discuss your ideas with a partner.

5 Imagine that the doctor pays the family a visit to see how they are getting on. How will Mother tell him about the jarrah trees? What will his reaction be? Write another story about what happens next. Think carefully about how each character might act and what they might say. You could develop this into an improvised drama.

6 Look closely at the structure of the story, and write a short description of the writer's techniques in shaping it, quoting from the text. For example:
- how does the writer engage the reader's interest in the characters at the beginning?
- how does she build tension?
- at what point in the story do you begin to guess that Mother has a plan to hold on to the land?
- what words and phrases does the writer use to prepare for the ending of the story?

My Parents

Before you read
1 Working in a small group, focus on one or both of your parents and brainstorm a list of their positive qualities.

What's it about?
Read the text and answer questions 2 to 4 by yourself. Then discuss your ideas in a small group.

2 What were Adrian Mitchell's mother's strongest characteristics?

3 What made his father speak very little?

4 'We all loved one another and this love was never shadowed.' What was the secret of the family's happiness?

Thinking about the text
5 The writer builds up a portrait of his parents through a series of sharply remembered anecdotes as well as description of their characteristics. Pick out four details that convey them most vividly to you, and write a paragraph to explain why.

6 Adrian Mitchell once said: 'My poems should ideally be spoken aloud . . . I want to talk as clearly as possible.' Try reading *My Parents* aloud in a small group, dividing it into sections and taking it in turns to read. Ask your audience for their response.

7 Write a piece about your own parents, using a similar style (that is, prose that uses poetic language). Use your list from question 1 to help you. You might mention:
- anecdotes that capture their characters
- typical habits
- physical appearance
- a sentence that sums up your relationship with them.

Would they be embarrassed to read it?

Forging a Family

Before you read

1. What do you think is the best advice for a family that wants to stick together? Discuss your ideas with a partner.

What's it about?

Read the text and answer questions 2 to 4 by yourself. Then compare your answers with a partner's.

2. Make a list of three things that Sue Palmer recommends in forging a family. Are any of them the same as your own advice in question 1? Is your list the same as your partner's?

3. What is 'slow time'? Do you have any in your family?

4. How do children develop 'an inner code of conduct' that guides and protects them?

Thinking about the text

5. Use Sue Palmer's suggestions as the basis of a questionnaire which you can use to find out about your friends' families. For example, one question could ask whether they eat together. Draw three tick boxes for each question – often / sometimes / hardly ever.

6. Imagine you are a parent drawing up 'basic rules' for family behaviour. What would be your top ten?

7. This piece is a good example of persuasive writing. What techniques does the author use to win us over? Write a short essay, quoting examples of the following techniques:
   - emotive language (language which creates a strong emotional response in the reader)
   - quoting the experts
   - positive examples
   - convincing reasons
   - repetition.

A Christmas Carol and *The Trouble Was Meals*

Before you read

1 What do you already know about Dickens? You may have seen TV, film or musical versions of some of his stories, and perhaps you know some of his characters. Pool your knowledge in a small group.

What's it about?

Read the story and the poem and answer questions 2 to 4 by yourself. Then compare your answers with a partner's.

2 Make a list of all the members of the large Cratchit family, adding any details about them from the story. Do the same for the family in the poem.

3 What words and phrases indicate that Dickens' story is set in the Victorian age?

4 Sum up the main difficulties caused by Grandma at mealtimes. Give examples from the poem.

Thinking about the text

5 Write two paragraphs emphasising the main differences in atmosphere between the two family meals in the texts. Think about the relationship between family members, and the levels of tension.

6 In a small group, and using your notes from question 2, create a tableau or freeze-frame of the Cratchit family at dinner. Try to convey as much as you can about each character and what they feel about each other. Then do the same for the family in the poem.

7 Choose one of the following two activities.
   a *A Christmas Carol*: Later on in the story, the Ghost of Christmas Future shows Scrooge what might happen if he doesn't help the Cratchits. Write a short piece describing the scene, or improvise it with a small group. Then compare your version with Dickens'.
   b *The Trouble Was Meals*: Improvise a meal after the death of Grandma. Think about whether Mother will miss her or not. What might the writer say about the bowl?

Compare and contrast

1 Who would you like in your family? Think back over all the texts in this section. Who sticks out in your mind as a very positive family member? Write a short piece explaining what you value about them.

2 In *Forging a Family*, Sue Palmer describes some of the elements that go towards making a happy family; for example, doing things together, shared interests, agreed rules. Which of the families in this section do you think gets closest to the ideal, and how? Discuss your ideas in a small group.

3 *An Overcrowded House* and *A Christmas Carol* both describe a family meal. Write a short piece comparing the two pieces, bringing out the similarities and differences. Think about:
- the reason for the meal
- who is there
- who cooks the food
- people's moods
- the tone and language of the piece.

4 The pieces in this section cover a wide range of text types, from Victorian novel to chatty letters. Choose three contrasting texts and write a short comparison, bringing out the differences in style, sentence structure and vocabulary. Which text do you prefer, and why?

2 Conflict and confusion

What did we do that was wrong?

Even the most perfect family has times when there are disagreements and when different members feel misunderstood. As a teenager, it's likely that you will begin to challenge your parents as you struggle for independence. They may have expectations for you which conflict with your own ambitions, and they may be bewildered by your opposition. Brothers and sisters too may often get on each other's nerves. In these circumstances it's hard to be reasonable and to appreciate different viewpoints. The pieces in this section illustrate how contradictory emotions can be at this stage.

Activities

1 Make a list of all the family disagreements you can remember in the last month or so. Try to group them into different categories; for example:
   - money
   - friends
   - attitudes
   - beliefs
   - privileges
   - other.

   Compare your list with a partner's. Are they similar? Can you explain the differences – for example, perhaps one of you is an only child, or perhaps one set of parents is stricter?

2 Think of a recent family argument. How did it start? Who was involved? Did it get resolved? How could it have been avoided? Make notes to share in a small group.

3 Working on your own or with a partner, make a list of ten Dos and Don'ts for the parents of teenagers. Then make similar lists for the teenagers.

Buried Treasure
by Chris Buckton

> This story comes from a collection called *The Giddy Limit!* (Ginn, 1990), describing my childhood nearly 60 years ago. My father and brother are both dead now, but writing stories about them is a way of keeping them alive in my mind.

Introduction

Sometimes I was glad that I was part of a big family. It meant that if you quarrelled with one of your brothers or sisters, there was always another one to side with you. We all had very different ways of looking at things, different ideas for doing things, so I hardly ever got bored. And never lonely. Even at school, where I had other friends, I still had that toast-warm feeling in the back of my mind that my family would be there in an emergency. It all sounds too happy to be true, doesn't it? What about the other times?

Times when you couldn't have something you wanted because there wasn't enough money after it had been divided by five.

When you really wanted to be on your own and there was nowhere to go.

When there always seemed to be someone in the loo when you wanted it.

When someone had 'borrowed' your pen or your best jersey.

When you couldn't have a bedroom to yourself.

When nobody noticed if you were really upset.

And especially when you couldn't finish a sentence without getting interrupted.

But I haven't told you our names or anything much about us. (You see, I even interrupt myself.) Tom came first, then me (I'm Polly), then Rachel, then Liz and last of all Mark. Most of these stories happened when I was about 12, so I guess Tom would have been about 14, Rachel 10, Liz 5 and Mark 2. We called Liz and Mark 'the little ones', because there was a big gap in age between Rachel and Liz. Rachel and I were often called 'the girls'. (Who by?

I can't remember, but I did quite like the name – it sounded grand and haughty.) Tom was just Tom, the eldest, the bully. He tormented me and I hated him for that, but still, I must admit, I did like it best of all when I was counted with him, when we were called 'the big two', leaving the others out. We lived in the country with plenty of space for exploring. In those days, towards the end of the 1940s, everywhere seemed safer and people didn't seem to worry if we went off by ourselves and made our own amusement.

Thinking about it now, it seems a perfect sort of childhood. At the time, of course, we often wished we lived in a city and we envied children who had more possessions.

'You're the giddy limit! You don't know how lucky you are,' my mother would say. 'I know you don't have much pocket money, but you have each other.'

I would pull a face behind my hair. Who could seriously prefer my brother to pocket money?

Buried treasure

When my brother Tom and I quarrelled, which was most of the time, I played with my sister Rachel. In fact, she and I did most things together. I took her for granted because she was younger than me and, looking back, I suppose I bullied her, just as much as Tom bullied me, although I did it in a different way. I used to betray her, too, because whenever Tom turned on his charm, I would drop whatever I was doing with Rachel to go off with him. I wonder if I was especially mean or whether everyone is a traitor like that?

Some of the best moments in the world, though, were being with Rachel. It was like being *with* yourself, less lonely than *by* yourself. She generally just tagged along and didn't talk much, which suited me because I talked all the time. She could be very obstinate though, and didn't always do what I wanted. She wouldn't argue, she'd just go silently stubborn.

She was much prettier than me and I was quite jealous of her. She had curly hair and a little pointed chin, big eyes, and a serene sort of smile. Her hands were delicate and always seemed to stay clean. My father once told me not to worry when I was feeling especially jealous. He said my hands might not be delicate, but they were very *useful* hands. It didn't make up for it at the time. Useful sounded ordinary.

Rachel and I shared a bedroom. I could never get straight to sleep. There were too many things to think over, worry about, or plan for the next day. As soon as I got into bed, I could feel my brain revving up instead of floating away. I hated it when Rachel fell asleep first, which she always did. I could see the peaceful hump that was her, faintly lifting up and down as she breathed, and I would feel a knot of loneliness starting in my stomach and slowly moving up my throat until I couldn't stay in bed any longer. I would creep out and shake the hump. I would shake it until it turned back into Rachel, a crotchety Rachel.

'Wassamatter?'

'Wake up. Listen. I've had an idea.'

'I'm too sleepy.' She was like a floppy doll with no bones in her body.

'Wake UP. *Listen.* Let's talk to each other in sound language. It won't count as talking so we won't get told off. But that way we can find out if the other person is still awake.'

Rachel wasn't enthusiastic. I couldn't really blame her. If I left her alone, then she would never need to know who was awake because she'd be asleep.

She made a noble effort. 'What's sound language? Words are sound language. I don't get it.' Her head lolled back and I gave her another shake.

'Don't act so stupid. I mean like a sort of code, so when we promise we won't talk, we can still communicate. Like this.' I made a series of little 'mm' noises in a rhythm – 'Mm-mm-mm-mm.'

'Wha'?'

'Mm-mm-mm-mm.'

Silence.

'Well, go on, guess what I'm saying.'

'How do *I* know?'

'Well use your INTELLIGENCE. Mm-mm-mm-mm. Hel-lo-Rach-el. Got it? Now, you try it.'

'Mm-mm-mm-mm. Mm-mm.'

I guessed. Easily. 'Hello Polly.' And I guessed the next bit too. 'Good night.' It worked. I tried something more ambitious. 'Mm-*MM*.' ('Wake UP.')

Silence.

'Mm-*MM*.'

Nothing.

'*MM-MM*.'

Then from downstairs, the sound of a door opening. Footsteps on the stairs.

'Are you still talking?'

'No. Rachel's asleep.'

'Well, you settle down too.' My mother's silhouette filled the doorway. We always left the door open so that the light from the landing would shine in. I wasn't exactly afraid of the dark, it was just that the dark seemed to bring wakeful, worrying thoughts – like everyone has to die, eventually, including me and Tim, my dog.

'I can't settle down. I can't get to sleep. It's so lonely being the last person in the world awake.'

'Well, you're not. Think of Australia and go to sleep.'

Instead of Australia I thought about codes, and dying. But this time the thought of dying didn't give me that horrible blank terror it usually gave me. In fact, it gave me a really good idea. Too good to waste on a sleepy Rachel. I would wait till the morning.

'A club. A 1946 club. Hundreds of years from now they'll find all the documents about it and the treasure we hide in the tin, and they'll be able to work out what life was really like, *is* like, now. They will wonder who buried it (we'll put it all in a rust-proof tin), so we could put in descriptions of ourselves – and we'll be remembered for ever. Or at least, our things will be remembered and we'll be of use to humanity.'

'What?'

'Well, we'll help them find out about the past.'

'But it isn't the past.'

'It will be then. When they find it.'

'We haven't got a rusty tin.'

'Rust-proof! The opposite of rusty.'

Sometimes Rachel was unbelievably slow-witted. She never, ever sounded really excited by any of my ideas. Why couldn't she, just once, leap up and down shouting, 'Brilliant, Polly, just BRILLIANT!'? Trying to get her involved in something was like trying to run in a muddy ploughed field. Her lip would curl a little bit, just flicker, her shoulders would shrug, and she would ask something practical, irritatingly down-to-earth. Irritating because it was generally something I hadn't thought of.

'We can find a tin somewhere. But first we've got to decide what to put in it.'

In my top drawer I had still got some pale blue writing paper and envelopes given to me by my Auntie Madge at Christmas. (Rather a hint *I* thought, but it hadn't worked, apart from the dull and dutiful thank-you letter which my mother forced me to write!) The paper lay crisp under a blue ribbon, ready for something special.

After a lot of argument we finally agreed that we'd each write down our name, age and address, followed by a description of ourself.

'We could even include a photograph or a drawing to show what we look like,' I suggested. 'For all we know, by the time it's found, the world might be populated by creatures from another planet, and human beings could be an extinct species.'

Rachel was not convinced – probably because her crayons needed sharpening and she couldn't be bothered. 'We don't need pictures. There will be television programmes and people will know everything from those.'

'What if there's a holocaust? Only things like our tin will survive. Film and TV sets would just melt.'

Rachel was worn down. She didn't even know what a holocaust was, but she agreed just for the sake of getting on with it.

After the description came hobbies. I put horse-riding, reading, drawing, acting, adventures, animals – and then, when Rachel wasn't looking, I added writing. I had recently written a play about Joan of Arc and a story about an Alsatian dog. Maybe years from now people would read them. It made me feel better about dying.

Rachel put down playing with toys and eating. She said she hadn't any more, but I suspect that was so she didn't have to write much.

Then I designed a title page, in my best fancy lettering:

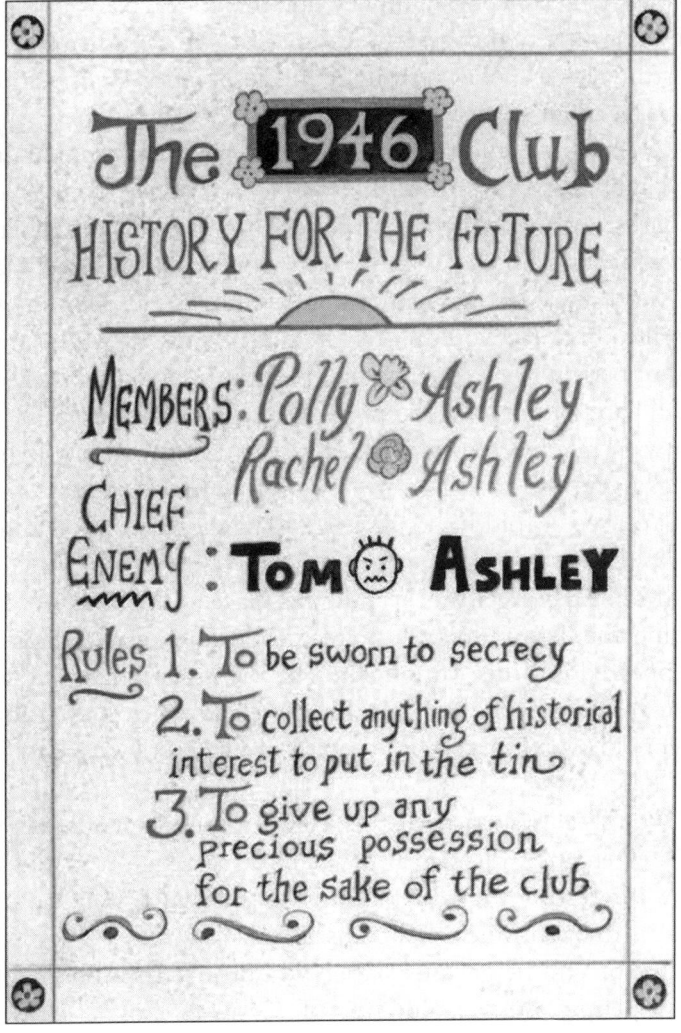

We got a biscuit tin easily enough, but working out what objects should go in it was really difficult. It was hard to guess which things would go on being ordinary and every day and therefore not at all interesting to dig up in a thousand years, and which things would be mysterious to anybody who wasn't alive now.

I remembered Tom finding a Roman coin once, and how amazing that was, imagining some Roman child in a tunic, maybe having it as pocket money, and then one day dropping it and being upset, and never guessing how we would find it in our strange world of electric light and aeroplanes. We must put in pocket money. But whose?

Rachel cried, and told *Tom* of all people, luckily not about The Club, just about me trying to take her money. Tom called me an extortioner which I had to look up in Dad's dictionary, and, while I was in Dad's study, I very carefully just hinted. Dad was very interested in history and I thought the idea might appeal to him. He wouldn't tell anyone because he wasn't that kind of person. He was gentle and thoughtful and had the very useful habit of not listening properly when our mother came to him with tales of our wickednesses. His mind was on higher things I suppose.

'You see,' I told him, 'we don't want money for spending. It's for the future.'

'Mm.' His finger was keeping his place in the book he was reading and he couldn't wait to magic me out of existence as he disappeared into his work again. He was a lecturer, so he was often at home working in his study. We had strict instructions never to disturb him except in emergencies. Mostly we forgot he was there.

'You see, I'm sorry to disturb you, but I think it could count as an emergency. Just a penny would do. Though it would be more interesting,' I added hastily as his hand went to his pocket, 'to have some other coins as well.'

In the end he gave us sixpence, a bronze threepenny bit, and a penny, plus an old copy of *The News Chronicle* with a headline about London being bombed. September 1940. The Blitz. (That was history already.)

I added two French coins left over from someone's holiday.

'Now,' I said to Rachel, 'clothes and things. How about a sandal? I've grown out of them so no one will notice.'

'And my hair ribbon and slide.'

'And your expanding silver bracelet.'

'No!' Rachel clutched on to it and her chin wobbled.

I gave in gracefully. 'You fat toad.'

'I'm not fat, I'm just plunk.'

'Plump, you idiot, but in fact you're FAT.'

She wasn't. She was smooth and round. Her knees in summer looked like two beautiful brown eggs. I was skinny; my knees looked like sticks. Why was I so jealous of her? Would I be pleased to get rid of her? Or would I save her from danger? Feelings were so muddled, they flooded over me, all tangled up with each other.

'Here.' She must have guessed my murderous thoughts. The bracelet dropped into the biscuit tin. By the time it was full and ready to bury, we added: Mum's last shopping list (instead of the actual items, which would have been missed), a *Thomas the Tank Engine* book, a copy of *The Radio Times* and a tin opener which I thought maybe might become a mystery object. I liked the idea of someone dressed in a space suit, turning it round and round trying to guess what on earth it could have been used for. By then they would be living on pills. We put in a tin of spam to give them a clue.

We buried the biscuit tin outside the playroom at the back of the flower bed. I dug while Rachel kept look-out, especially for Chief Enemy. Liz and Mark, the little ones, came to watch, but that didn't matter. Mark couldn't talk properly yet, and Liz didn't really understand what it was all about.

'Polly, Polly, what are you doing?'

'Digging the garden. Putting in a plant.'

'Pa pa.' Mark scattered soil everywhere.

'Can I help?' asked Liz. 'That's not a plant.'

'Yes it is.' I covered up the biscut tin as fast as I could.

'Will it grow biscuits?' She wasn't as stupid as I'd supposed. I would have to bribe her.

'Bikki?' echoed Mark hopefully. 'Bikki?'

'Would you like to borrow my best book?' I was so busy getting rid of Liz and Mark that I didn't hear Rachel's yelp until she came running, still yelping – 'He's coming, he's coming!'

The tin stuck out, he would be bound to see it. I scrabbled in the soil and got it out.

'Quick! I'll stop him and you hide it in the playroom.' I pushed it into Rachel's hands, and turned. Round the corner came Tom. Rachel was just disappearing through the playroom door, so I ran after her, slammed the door behind us and leaned against it to stop Tom.

The next thing I knew, there was a shattering crash of glass, the sight of Tom's hand appearing on *my* side of the door, a scream from somewhere and blood dripping onto the playroom floor. Terror made us all stay quite still for a moment, as if we were having our photograph taken. Tom stared at his hand. Then he seemed to wake up. 'I've cut an artery,' he said calmly, and, as he pulled his hand back through the splintered glass, there was the clatter of more glass falling out. 'Get Mum.'

Mum took one look, put her finger on the cut to stop the pumping blood, and bundled Tom into the car. Funny that such a fussy person could be so calm in a crisis. 'Look after the little ones while I take Tom to hospital. Your father's in his study.'

It gave us a chance to finish burying the biscuit tin. We had to do it twice, though, because the first time Mark saw us, and when we'd finished he just stood there pointing to the spot saying, 'Bikki, bikki.'

'NO BIKKI!' I said, so fiercely that it made him cry. I took a biscuit from the kitchen cupboard to shut him up, and while he was happily chomping, we finally completed our mission in a different place so that Mark wouldn't be able to give it away. Then, of course, Liz wanted a biscuit, and that made Rachel and I so hungry we couldn't resist. It was an ABSOLUTE RULE NEVER TO TAKE FOOD – I suppose that wartime rationing had made it seem much more important than it might seem now. Of course, if we had the chance, we got tempted beyond endurance. It seemed that we were always hungry. I don't mean seriously hungry, just desperately peckish. There was never enough money for snacks, and pocket-money sweets didn't last long. Our mother called it stealing, which I suppose it was, and whenever she baked a batch of buns, she'd tell us she knew how many she'd made, to stop us lifting one.

We sat on the kitchen door-step munching biscuits and thinking about Tom. I had a horrible foggy feeling in my head whenever I thought about it. Guilt. What if he bled to death? I had done it, I had slammed the door. What if he couldn't use his hand properly any more? Every day I would see it and be reminded that it was my fault. He wanted to be a cricketer, his career would be ruined. Oh Tom! I didn't hate him at all. I didn't mind how often he bullied me, I just wanted him back and all right again so that the fog in my head could lift.

When the car came back, and Tom climbed out with only a little bandage, and a smug smile on his face, I was so relieved I ran down the path and hugged him. He was as surprised as I was.

But our adventures never ended happily ever after. 'Polly! Where have all the biscuits gone? And just *look* at Mark.' He must have found the tin of chocolate ones while I had been sitting worrying.

'Bikki,' he said through a smeary face. 'All gone bikki.'

'How *can* you be so selfish? *You* cause an accident, Tom is badly cut, and all you can do is sit there eating. Don't you care about Tom at all?'

My mouth opened to protest, but what was the use? How could she be so blind? I had *hugged* him.

Tom caught my eye. *He* knew.

That biscuit tin is probably still there today, buried in that garden. But I'll tell you a secret. The future won't find a tin of spam. Another day, we got tempted beyond endurance.

Further reading

There are many other childhood memoirs you might enjoy, such as *Jacky Daydream* (Corgi Yearling Books, 2008) by the popular author of teenage fiction Jacqueline Wilson.

A Parents' and Teenagers' Alphabet Book
by David Crystal

> David Crystal is one of the world's best-known language experts. The experience of bringing up four children might have inspired this poem.

*They're aggravating
    belly-aching
    crying out loud and always
    driving up the wall.

*They're edgy
    fractious
    grouchy and always getting on a
    high horse.

*They're insufferable
    juvenile, don't
    keep their hair on and always
    laying down the law.

*They're maddening
    never satisfied
    opinionated and always
    pointing the finger.

*They're quick-tempered
    ratty
    sulky and always ready to
    take offence.

*They're uncooperative
    very scratchy
    wearing and always e
    xtremely moody.

And

*They're unsociable and
    boring.

Parents/Teenagers (delete to taste)

But those last two lines don't begin with Y and Z that's just what I'd expect from you you can't even be bothered to find a couple of lousy words when it's me we're talking about two words that's all I don't think you care two hoots about my feelings you never listen anyway so what's the point in saying anything it isn't possible to have a proper conversation with you any more and while we're talking as a matter of fact I've got a bone to pick with you . . .

Further reading

You can find out more about David Crystal from his entertaining blog (visit http://www.david-crystal.blogspot.com). Many of his articles about language are published on the Internet, some of them with intriguing titles like *Never Bolt Your Door with a Boiled Carrot* (visit http://www.fifthestate.co.uk and search for 'boiled carrot').

Urgent Note to My Parents
by Hiawyn Oram

> Hiawyn Oram has been writing children's books and television scripts for more than 20 years and has published over 60 books. You can probably tell that this poem was written by someone with experience of teenage children: Oram has two grown-up sons.

Don't ask me to do what I can't do
Only ask me to do what I can
Don't ask me to be what I can't be
Only ask me to be what I am

Don't one minute say 'Be a big girl'
And the next 'You're too little for that'
PLEASE don't ask me to be where I can't be
PLEASE be happy with right where I'm at

Further reading
Hiawyn Oram has written many popular picture books for young children, including *Angry Arthur* (Anderson Press Ltd, 2008), a vivid portrayal of a child's tantrum, and the *Mona the Vampire* books (Orchard Books), which have been made into a BBC TV series.

One Small Step

by Shyama Perera

> Shyama Perera was born in Moscow where her father was a diplomat. In 1962 her family came to London and her father left them. This story about Mala is based around Shyama's stormy adolescence in Paddington with her determined mother.

It's one of those dates that sticks in your memory forever: the twenty-first of July 1969. Thinking back, it was the week the summer holidays started, but the days that followed have left no imprint. What I remember about the twenty-first of July was that man walked on the moon.

I was almost twelve and my Auntie Rishi was throwing a party to celebrate her engagement to a toothy man with the darkest skin who'd come from Sri Lanka...

Ma had said I could wear my new dress: blue-and-brown check with a hooped zip that ran from belly button to neck. 'Groovy' we called it in those days: 'That's a seriously groovy dress, Mala.' It was very grown up, actually. Which was unusual because we were younger for longer then, if that makes sense. We believed in ghosts... and witches and fairies right up until the moment when secondary school robbed us of innocence and threw us into a world of new terminology: smocks, sox, wet-look boots, sex, drugs and rock 'n' roll.

That same day, my friend Janice's older sister, Allie, had come round after school and talked about free love. Someone had written FREE LOVE – just like that, in huge black capitals – on the white wall outside the estate agent's on the corner.

'Well, it's the rage, innit, free love?' Allie said, adjusting a slingback stiletto. 'Be who you are, be who you want, with who *you* want. Let it all hang out. Hang free.'

Afterwards, my mum bristled in her nylon sari. 'I don't want that girl coming into this room again, Mala. These westerners.

Chi! Free love? Don't they know that nothing in this world is free? That everything comes with a price?'

She slapped the roti[1] dough harder and harder on to the Formica work surface in the little alcove that passed for a kitchen in the Paddington tenements. 'Janice should know better than to listen to that nonsense. You should know better! Hippy-chippy, what use is any of this if she can't even get five O levels?'

Part of me, the sensible part, agreed. But there was a new voice in my head that questioned everything Ma believed in. Allie wasn't a slapper by any stretch of the imagination. Peter Gill's sister had slept with half the red watch from Warwick Avenue fire station, and Kelly Grey's sister, Mary, was up the duff by a *black* man. The whole street was in a flap, including my mother who claimed she didn't dislike black men any more than she disliked all men, but nonetheless his colour was added to her catalogue of complaint.

'You see, this is how they end up, black and white. From the gutter they drag themselves further down, into the sewer. You say I'm old-fashioned, Mala, but we Asians have moral codes. We understand that nothing in life is easy, and we are prepared to work for it.'

'But my dad ran away, and he was Asian.'

My mother didn't answer as she rolled out the roti dough and cut rounds using a teacup. I knew that Allie was far too sensible to end up like Mary Grey, but Ma was convinced that girls bought the birth-control pill on street corners the way hippies bought hashish on Portobello Road on a sunny Saturday afternoon.

'If these girls buy the pill, they won't get pregnant will they, Ma?' I said.

'How do you know about these things?'

'So they're clever girls, not stupid?'

'Mala, I don't want to hear you say these things! Is this what Allie says? I wish you didn't mix with that family.'

---

[1] **roti**   a type of flatbread

Lovely Allie, such an enigma to my mother who, alone in a strange country, had developed a fear of the unknown. She saw so much she didn't like or understand and she didn't want to get any closer – to risk infection. But she'd got it wrong about Allie, who was fifteen, fearless and straight as a die. Sometimes Allie would let me and Janice hang around with her, and she taught us things.

'I enjoy the chase with guys, but I don't let them in for the kill,' she told us one afternoon, walking up to Paddington Station. 'Act mean and keep 'em keen. When I lose it, it'll be to someone special. You be the same when you grow up, all right? Silly to chuck it away on a fumble with some idiot behind a wall on North Wharf Road.'

Pulling on my new checked dress, I gave up arguing with my mum. She had fixed views on everything, from Harold Wilson to the price of the eels that were kept, alive, in giant white tubs outside the local MacFisheries. But I couldn't resist rubbing her up the wrong way one last time. After all, another ten weeks and I'd be twelve – the oldest girl in my new class, probably. I should be able to ask important questions.

'Ma, do you think Allie's the sort of girl who goes topless at Woodstock?'

'Chi! All these western girls showing their breasts! They have no shame. No decorum. In our home country, Mala, a woman is a . . . woman.'

'But we're here, Ma, not home.'

'That doesn't mean you have to take on their terrible ways. It is possible for you to enjoy the best of both worlds.'

The best of both worlds! I wasn't even getting the best of *one* world. My entire life, it seemed to me, was a series of chores, interspersed with homework and warnings about situations I didn't even recognize, let alone experience.

My mother sniffed to herself as the rotis cooked. 'It starts in America; soon it will come here.'

'What?'

'Pop concerts. You hear my words. Peace and love.'

She said 'peace and love' like you'd say 'Jack the Ripper' or 'increased income tax'. But those words fuelled us. All of us kids greeted each other with a two-fingered salute: 'Peace and love, man.' Peace and love. It was beautiful!

Mum's voice receded to a background drone as I admired my dress in the mirror. I was filled with excitement. Rishi's getting married, and tonight Neil Armstrong will land Apollo 11 on the moon! How fantastic. How *bloody* fantastic.

It seems so far away now. Because nobody's walked on the moon since then. Not one footstep more in over thirty years. Sting sang a song about it: *Giant steps are what you take, walking on the moon*. Giant steps: they looked more like bounces really – like the Clangers – when I watched the walk on TV the next day.

It's strange. They've sent probes to Mars and to Venus and there are space stations circling this planet every twenty-four hours. We operate satellites that can see into each and every room of any house in the world and eavesdrop on every single telephone call. But every time there's footage of man walking on the moon, it's the same footage that I would see for the first time that summer of '69.

That night, on the threshold of puberty, on the verge of upgrading from child to pre-teen, nothing could have been more exciting than the NASA space expedition. Perhaps thinking about it now, it was because man was entering uncharted territory – just as my mother had done by bringing me to England. To the big rooming houses of Paddington where my father had put us up in a bedsit, sharing a bath and toilet with the occupants of thirteen other rooms, before disappearing into the ether, just like that. He'd left Ma alone and unsupported, to raise me. But that was *her* uncharted territory, and while she was a stranger in a strange land, trying to find a path forwards, I was a citizen of that strange land and everything looked utterly straight and simple to me.

Except that soon I too would embark on an unknown journey, swapping gobstoppers and Lucky Bags for spots, boys and hours of homework. For David Bowie, Roxy Music and Showaddywaddy.

Ma took the rotis off the two-ring Baby Belling electric stove that was fitted in identikit bedsits around the city. The little window was open and the milk she'd left on the sill to keep cold looked curdled. 'Eat now, or you'll be waiting till nine to be fed. Now Rishi has a man to run behind, we may not eat at all.'
'Is it an arranged marriage?'
'Nothing is arranged.'
'I mean, did their parents introduce them?'
'They're old enough to introduce themselves, Mala. The woman is nearly thirty, for goodness' sake. Why don't you concern yourself with more important matters?'
'Like what?'
She didn't answer, tightening her lips instead and popping the plate on my knees as I sat on the bed.

Everyone was at Rishi's: Anu, Seeli, Vimala, Shanthi, Oliver, Manel, Prisky, Palitha . . . There was a baila[2] tape playing noisily, and Auntie Lata was doing an arm-flapping dance to its calypso rhythm and singing along: *Malu, malu, malu* – fish, fish, fish.
   She was not the only entertainment. Everyone was watching Rishi's boyfriend, Arthur. In honesty, he wasn't quite as awful as he'd looked in the photographs that had been passed round at a recent reception at the Commonwealth Institute.
   The teeth were still oversized, but a brilliant white, and now that the legs were also on view, the belly was more a pillow than a barrel. As Arthur's laugh boomed across the room, everyone was hooked.

---

[2]**baila**   Sri Lankan dance music

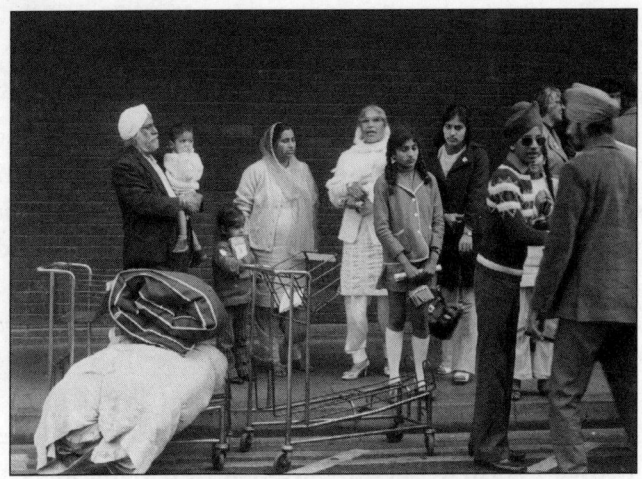
An Asian family arriving in England, circa 1969.

Spotting my mother deep in conversation with Vimala, I scooted over, but they immediately slipped into Sinhalese. Whatever they were saying, it had to be good!

'Not everything is appropriate for the ears of children, Mala,' Ma said when I challenged her.

'But I'm not *children*, I'm nearly twelve. I'm me.'

'Why don't you find a book to read?'

'What? The Bible?'

My mother coloured at this because Auntie Rishi was Christian, and I'd said the name of their holy book in the same disdainful voice my mother used in private.

'Please don't be rude. You're becoming a scallywag.'

'Then *you* don't be rude and talk in Sinhalese. It's no different to whispering.' I knew I'd overstepped the mark here, but she could hardly give me a slap with everyone around us. 'You're probably talking about sex again,' I added archly. 'Who cares if Rishi looked flushed when we called round here on Saturday?'

My mother had developed hot spots on her cheeks. 'Be quiet. What's got into you tonight, child? Do you want to upset every single person in this place?'

I looked at her mutinously. 'But I heard you say that.'
Now Vimala joined in. 'You and your mother live in one room, Mala. Sometimes you'll hear things you shouldn't. You must judge what is appropriate and what isn't.'

... I turned my back crossly on my mother and Vimala, not wanting a replay of past misdemeanours, and exited rapidly through the nearest door, to find myself in Rishi's backyard.

Around me the houses of Gloucester Terrace loomed disproportionately in relation to the small handkerchief of garden space. These days they'd probably call it a patio and charge some unknowing fool a million pounds for the privilege of putting their pots in it, but our part of West London was grotty in those days. A yard was a yard.

Most of the houses in the area were owned by a Sikh conglomerate. They rented them mainly to white people but there were some other Asians around – people like us, who'd pitched up from nowhere and felt like nothings. Well, my mother felt like nothing, anyway. She felt conspicuous in her sari and she said we smelt like 'curry puffs' because we lived in one room and the odour of cooking stuck to our clothes despite endless airing. London was cranking up for the bouts of racial violence that became known as 'Paki bashing' and Ma sensed the growing tension. The burden of responsibility made her old before her time. But it wasn't an anxiety I shared because England was all I'd known, really. I was part of it, not apart from it.

'You mustn't draw attention to yourself, Mala.'
'All I did was say good morning to the bus conductor.'
'One day the bus conductor will spit in your eye.'
'Why?'
'Because we're different and they don't like us.'
'Then let's make them like us.'

Once, when I was waiting for her outside a shop, a lady stopped and asked where I came from. I said Sri Lanka. She smiled and replied, 'Ah, Sri Lanka, such a lovely country. Why don't you go back there?'

I'd thought the woman was nice and chatty. Ma said she was a Powellite: a follower of the MP Enoch Powell who claimed having immigrants in Britain would lead to rivers 'foaming with much blood'. No wonder Ma was always scared . . .

By ten, the party was warming up. The peach wine was flowing and even Ma was a little giggly. But I stayed in the yard, cheesed off at my exclusion from gossip and revelry.

Luckily, Arthur had taken the TV outside because it improved the reception from the small set-top aerial. I switched it on. *Ready Steady Go!* was the only programme I enjoyed – like *Top of the Pops* but cooler. Really. They had this serious babe called Cathy McGowan with brown hair to her waist and the shortest dresses and the whitest boots. She'd sit there giggling with the big stars like Adam Faith and Georgie Fame and Tom Jones. The Rolling Stones played live. But tonight it was just the usual serious stuff – God or politics or African rhino or something – and despite the TV being outside, there was still a snowstorm across the screen.

I banged the set – a completely acceptable cure at the time – and then kicked at the paving stones angrily because the picture started strobing instead. I was filled with a sudden anger – and I focused it on Ma because it felt like everything that went wrong in my life was her fault. I hate my *bloody* mother, I thought. Why does she treat me like some moron who doesn't understand what's going on?

As I stood seething, the ultimate horror happened: bossy Auntie Anu came out. 'How are you doing at school, Mala?'

'Fine.'

'Looking forward to a new start in September?'

'Sort of.'

'It's fantastic that you got into a grammar school. Don't waste it.'

'I haven't even *started*!'

'You must work very hard and reward your mother's efforts.'

'They were *my* efforts.'

'Don't be stupid – your mother has given up everything for you.'

'She hasn't given up nagging.'

'For goodness' sake grow up, Mala.'

'I'm *trying*!'

'A good education will pay your bills.'

'I don't have any bills.'

'Why are you so difficult, Mala? Always you sound as if you're speaking in exclamation marks. Is it too much to ask of you that you study hard and use your education instead of wasting it?'

Education: it was all I ever heard. Education was going to save me from an impoverished future cleaning toilets or selling nylon tights in Woolworth's. Big deal! It wasn't that I didn't believe it. It was just that the advice was taking on the rhythm of a mantra: school-learning-job-money-school-learning-job-money. Oh, yawn. If they didn't watch it, George Harrison would take the words to India on his next visit to the Maharishi Mahesh Yogi and turn it into a Beatles song... Crossly, I went back inside the flat.

'Ah, Mala! Long time, no see. Doing well at school, I hear.'

'Yes, Uncle Oliver.'

'And what will you study at university? Medicine, perhaps? Law?'

'I'm eleven years old.'

'Never too young to plan for the future.'

Crosser still, I went and sat in a corner, on one of the leather chairs bought at great expense from Frederick Lawrence. With her leather furniture and new gold Humber car, Rishi was a good catch. She was a doctor who'd intended returning home after her studies, but, when the time came, enjoyed the freedom of London too much to give it up. Now she said she was happy to sign away that freedom to Arthur, a man from a good family who designed bridges. Dental bridges as it turned out, but I didn't know that till later. His overbite wasn't the finest clue.

My mother called me over. Reluctantly, I went.

'Why doesn't anybody ever say anything nice?'

'What are you talking about, child?' She picked a fish cutlet from the table and popped it into my open mouth. 'Rishi has made them with tuna instead of mackerel, but they're very nice.'

'I'm always being asked about school.'

'You should be happy that people show an interest.'

'Why can't they ask me about other things?'

'Because going to school, Mala, is what you *do*.'

Somewhere inside I knew talking to me about school was no different to grown-ups talking to each other about work, but I resented it. Because the endless lectures always allied study to me being different from the majority of kids: an immigrant. As an immigrant, apparently, education was extra-important because it was my only escape from poverty and discrimination, and the powerlessness they bestow.

'You've been blessed with brains, Mala,' Ma would say.

'But if I'm really that clever, why do you keep repeating everything as if I can't remember from the last time?'

'In this country, you are nothing. Just a coloured face with no status. You have to go out and earn it.'

'Everyone has to go out and earn it.'

'But it's harder for you.'

I hated that. It made me feel like I had a disability or a hideous disfigurement that made me less capable of achievement . . .

My skin was my badge of identity: a declaration of my history and my culture. An additional point in the game of success. I thought everything about me was terrific. (And I knew the red-headed boy from Carroll House thought so too because he always winked when I walked past.) But Ma was experiencing life on the periphery of British society, with people who considered her 'other'. I was growing up alongside those people, and if they were sometimes rude or ignorant I just put them right. I saw myself absolutely as their equal, their colleague – and, usually, their friend.

Taking a handful of the fish cutlets, which really were delicious, I mooched off to a quiet corner. Not that it was quiet for long. This time it was my Auntie Prisky who cornered me.

'Your mother says you don't want to talk about school, Mala.'

'No, I don't.'

'What would you like to talk about? Boys? Is there someone you have a crush on?'

'No!'

She laughed. 'Methinks the lady doth protest too much. What's happened to Nicholas Titchener – wasn't that his name?'

I blushed furiously. 'I never liked Nicholas Titchener!' It wasn't quite a lie. I never liked him – he was a show-off and he'd kissed Debbie Flint in the playground. But I *loved* him. And it was my business – alone.

'Then let's discuss your hobbies, Mala. Do you still keep that Stanley Gibbons stamp catalogue? Do you still spend your pocket money on facsimiles?'

'Stamps are babyish.'

'Nothing to replace stamps? Perhaps not. Is Janice still your best friend?'

'Yes.'

'And her sister. What's her name?'

'Allie.'

'Yes, Allie. I see her sometimes loafing around, flirting with boys outside the Stowe Club. She must be nearly fifteen.'

'She's already fifteen.'

'A very pretty girl. But don't grow up like her. Are you planning any summer adventures with Janice?'

'Yes, we're going shopping in Whiteleys.'

Prisky ignored the sarcasm. 'You know there's a big summer mural project at the library?'

'Boring.'

Prisky sighed. 'It seems to me, Mala, people talk to you about school because it's impossible to discuss anything else.'

I didn't like this. I got up and prowled the room. I heard Prisky tell my mother that she thought I was hormonal and there was lots of laughter. I knew it was about periods . . .

Around midnight, tired and bored, I wandered outside again and saw these magical words on the screen: *Man has landed on the moon.* I read them again and again. *Man has landed on the moon. Man has landed on the moon.* MAN HAS LANDED ON THE MOON!

For that millisecond, as the enormity of it sank in, and before I ran inside screeching with excitement, my heart stopped. The memory brings a lump to my throat even now. Because science was so fresh to me, and everything from the clothes we wore to the music we played to the cars we drove was about pushing ideas to their limits. Each new achievement moved me. I was wild with the joy of it! And the adults were too. They streamed out into the yard and we all just stared at the screen, filled with wonder.

The next morning Neil Armstrong took his first step and put himself on the map and human beings firmly in the greater universe with the immortal words: 'One small step for man, a giant step[3] for mankind.' America had won the space race. The Russians had given us Yuri Gagarin, the first man in space. Now the Yanks had one-upped them in the most spectacular fashion. The achievement was as much about politics as science, but I didn't realize that then.

And for me, it had an importance beyond history. It is my first remembered stepping stone: a giant step for mankind, and a giant step for Mala too. I knew my whole life was about to change. That I was going to enter the adult world, albeit in a minor role, and that the things I did and the decisions I made in the years to come would colour my life forever. It brought me out in goosebumps.

---

[3] **step** 'leap' is the word Armstrong actually used here, as he stepped onto the moon

Over the next few years, as I started to juggle all my different interests and priorities – exams and romance, music and make-up, clothes and hobbies – I was a little more circumspect about what I said to whom. I learned it was better to rehearse arguments than lose my flow and my advantage in the heat of the moment. My ma and I battled less, though I still had trouble giving in, even when I knew I was wrong.

I think everyone, everywhere, associated that night with a global coming-of-age. We moved from the realms of fantasy to reality: from chemistry sets in the front room to real science, real technology, real adventure. If we could walk on the moon then anything was possible. I believed it then, and I believe it now.

That night I even saw my mother filled with a fantastic optimism. 'If we can conquer planets, Mala, there is no excuse for ignoring the problems of earth, which are much easier to resolve.'

On the way home, she stopped at a chocolate machine and bought two bars of Galaxy. We sat on the stairs outside our room at one in the morning, savouring the taste.

The next day, Janice and I perched on the wall, straddling the words FREE LOVE, and talked about it all.

'It's funny, isn't it?' Jan said. 'It's not really anything to do with us, but it's exciting. Like when President Kennedy got shot.'

'That was awful. My mum cried.'

'So did mine. Because they're Irish Americans. Like us.'

'You're not American.'

'We're Irish. That's enough.'

She pulled on her liquorice bootlace. 'This is the first day of the rest of our lives. Six weeks' time, you and me will be in different schools, with different friends and different interests.'

'Don't say that. You'll always be my friend.'

'That's what Allie and her mates said to each other four years ago, but it wasn't true.' She sighed as tears welled in my eyes. 'Another year and Allie'll get a job. She'll end up with a baby and then what? Decades of the same. Just like my mum: four kids, family allowance on Monday and a chip-pan fire every Friday because she's watching Mike Yarwood. That's growing up.'

I was momentarily silenced by her profound observation. 'We don't have to go the same way. *You* don't have to go the same way. Stop sounding like Eeyore. My mum says girls in the West lose their innocence too quickly. Don't be so old.'

'That isn't what your mum means by innocence.'

'I don't care what *she* means! I know what I mean.'

'I hate being a kid,' Janice said.

'It's better than being a grown-up, though. Isn't it?'

'I don't know. Ask me again in ten years' time.'

'By then people will be living on the moon. We could emigrate.'

'And neither of us would be strange or stupid or different. Would your mum let you, Mala?'

'Not unless I'd got my A levels.'

We started to laugh. 'It's great that we've got men on the moon, isn't it?' Janice said.

I nodded. 'Yeah. It's the most important thing that ever happened.'

Further reading

Shyama Perera has written four novels, including *Haven't Stopped Dancing Yet* (Sceptre, 1999), which tells the story of four girls growing up in 1960s London.

Independence
by Anne Frank

> Anne Frank was a Jewish girl who wrote a diary while she was in hiding with her family and four friends during the German occupation of the Netherlands in World War II. They hid in a small secret annexe behind her father's office building in Amsterdam. In August 1944 they were betrayed. Anne died in a concentration camp at Belsen, not knowing that her wish 'to go on living after my death' was to come true with the publication of her diary.
>
> It was hard for a lively teenager, struggling to become independent. She couldn't go out or have much privacy. She was cut off from friends of her own age, and invented 'Kitty' to take their place, writing to her about the stresses of her unusual life. Gradually she and Peter, their friends' son, became aware of a growing love for each other. But Anne's father, who she called Pim, disapproved . . .

Friday, 5 May 1944

Dear Kitty,

Father's unhappy with me. After our talk on Sunday he thought I'd stop going upstairs every evening. He won't have any of that *'Knutscherei'*[1] going on. I can't stand that word. Talking about it was bad enough – why does he have to make me feel bad too! I'll have a word with him today. Margot gave me some good advice. Here's more or less what I'd like to say:

'I think you expect an explanation from me, Father, so I'll give you one. You're disappointed in me, you expected more restraint from me, you no doubt want me to act the way a fourteen-year-old is supposed to. But that's where you're wrong!

'Since we've been here, from July 1942 until a few weeks ago, I haven't had an easy time. If only you knew how much I used to

---

[1] ***Knutscherei*** the German word for 'necking' or 'snogging'

cry at night, how unhappy and despondent I was, how lonely I felt, you'd understand my wanting to go upstairs! I've now reached the point where I don't need the support of Mother or anyone else. It didn't happen overnight. I've struggled long and hard and shed many tears to become as independent as I am now. You can laugh and refuse to believe me, but I don't care. I know I'm an independent person, and I don't feel I need to account to you for my actions. I'm only telling you this because I don't want you to think I'm doing things behind your back. But there's only one person I'm accountable to, and that's me.

'When I was having problems, everyone – and that includes you – closed their eyes and ears and didn't help me. On the contrary, all I ever got were admonitions not to be so noisy. I was noisy only to keep myself from being miserable all the time. I was over-confident to keep from having to listen to the voice inside me. I've been putting on an act for the last year and a half, day in, day out. I've never complained or dropped my mask, nothing of the kind, and now... now the battle is over. I've won! I'm independent, in both body and mind. I don't need a mother any more, and I've emerged from the struggle a stronger person.

'Now that it's over, now that I know the battle has been won, I want to go my own way, to follow the path that seems right to me. Don't think of me as a fourteen-year-old, since all these troubles have made me older; I won't regret my actions, I'll behave the way I think I should!

'Gentle persuasion won't keep me from going upstairs. You'll either have to forbid it, or trust me through thick and thin. Whatever you do, just leave me alone!'
Yours, Anne M. Frank

Saturday, 6 May 1944

Dearest Kitty,
    Last night before dinner I tucked the letter I'd written into Father's pocket. According to Margot, he read it and was upset for the rest of the evening. (I was upstairs washing up!) Poor Pim, I might have known what the effect of such an epistle

would be. He's so sensitive! I immediately told Peter not to ask any questions or say anything more. Pim's said nothing else to me about the matter. Is he going to?

Everything here is more or less back to normal. We can hardly believe what Jan, Mr Kugler and Mr Kleiman tell us about the prices and the people on the outside . . . People are paying 14.00 guilders an ounce for Bulgarian tobacco! . . . Break-ins, murders and thefts are daily occurrences. Even the police and night watchmen are getting in on the act. Everyone wants to put food in their stomachs, and since wages have been frozen, people have had to resort to swindling. The police have their hands full trying to track down the many girls of fifteen, sixteen, seventeen and older who are reported missing every day . . .

Yours, Anne M. Frank

Anne and Pim (centre).

Sunday morning, 7 May 1944

Dearest Kitty,
    Father and I had a long talk yesterday afternoon. I cried my eyes out, and he cried too. Do you know what he said to me, Kitty?
    'I've received many letters in my lifetime, but none as hurtful as this. You, who have had so much love from your parents. You, whose parents have always been ready to help you, who have always defended you, no matter what. You talk of not having to account to us for your actions! You feel you've been wronged and left to your own devices. No, Anne, you've done us a great injustice!
    'Perhaps you didn't mean it that way, but that's what you wrote. No, Anne, *we* have done nothing to deserve such a reproach!'
    Oh, I've failed miserably. This is the worst thing I've ever done in my entire life. I used my tears to show off, to make myself seem important so he'd respect me. I've certainly had my share of unhappiness, and everything I said about Mother is true. But to accuse Pim, who's so good and who's done everything for me – no, that was too cruel for words.
    It's good that somebody has finally cut me down to size, has broken my pride, because I've been far too smug. Not everything Mistress Anne does is good! Anyone who deliberately causes such pain to someone they say they love is despicable, the lowest of the low!
    What I'm most ashamed of is the way Father has forgiven me; he said he's going to throw the letter in the stove, and he's being so nice to me now, as if *he* were the one who'd done something wrong. Well, Anne, you still have a lot to learn. It's time you made a beginning, instead of looking down on other people and always blaming them!
    I've known a lot of sorrow, but who hasn't at my age? I've been putting on an act, but was hardly even aware of it. I've felt lonely, but never desperate! Not like Father, who once ran out into the street with a knife so he could put an end to it all. I've never gone that far.

I should be deeply ashamed of myself, and I am. What's done can't be undone, but at least you can keep it from happening again. I'd like to start all over again, and that shouldn't be difficult, now that I have Peter. With him supporting me, I *know* I can do it! I'm not alone any more. He loves me, I love him, I have my books, my writing and my diary. I'm not all that ugly, or that stupid, I have a sunny disposition, and I want to develop a good character!

Yes, Anne, you knew full well that your letter was unkind and untrue, but you were actually proud of it! I'll take Father as my example once again, and I *will* improve myself.

Yours, Anne M. Frank

Further reading

After reading the rest of Anne Frank's diary (Penguin Books Ltd, 2007), you might enjoy *Zlata's Diary* by Zlata Filipović (Penguin Books, 2006). Zlata was an 11-year-old who experienced the horrors of war in Sarajevo in the early 1990s.

Getting the Messages
by Anne Fine

> Anne Fine has won many awards and was Children's Laureate from 2001 to 2003. She is well known for her sharp humour, depth of feeling and challenging subject matter. This short story is taken from the collection *Very Different* (Mammoth, 2001), in which Anne Fine demonstrates her skills as a short story writer. The hero is wrestling with a dilemma – how to tell his parents what almost everybody else seems to know already . . .

How did I tell them? How does anybody tell them? It was a mixture of chance, and being up to here with the sheer awfulness of them not having a clue. (I'm not kidding. I don't think it had even crossed their minds.) I was a wreck from walking through our back door every day after school, practically expecting to see their pale shocked faces raised to mine. Sooner or later one of life's meddlers was going to take a swing at them with the old wet sock of truth, and come out with a helpful little 'I really thought it was time someone told you.' After all, most of my friends knew. And once Mr Heffer had soft-soled his way up behind me in the newsagent's while I was flicking through something pretty dubious, I was pretty sure all the staff were in on it (and half the dinner ladies, if that strange rumour about Mr Heffer has any truth to it). I even reckoned Mr Faroy the grocer had guessed, and I'm not sure he even knows quite what we're talking about.

So that just left them, really. Mum and Dad.

Like everyone else, though, I kept putting it off, not just from cowardice, but from not being sure quite what was driving me towards the dread day of reckoning. I wouldn't be surprised if axe-murderers have the same problem. They escape undetected from the scene of the crime, and then each knock, each phone ring, causes such a rush of stomach-clenching fear that in the end they realise one day soon they're going to walk into some police station – any police station – and give themselves up, just to be able to stretch out on their hard prison bed, and breathe in peace.

Not the best reason for confessing, perhaps. But good enough. And better than some of the others, like wanting to stop your parents making their tired old jokes about gay presenters on the telly, or simply upset them out of childish spite.

And I certainly didn't want to upset mine. I'm very fond of them, I really am. (Go on. Have a good laugh. I'll wait till you're ready.) I think they're both softies, if you want to know. And I'm the light of Mum's life. Even at my age, they're still checking on me all the time. 'All right, are you, son?' 'Good day at school, sweetheart?' That sort of thing. Not that I'm actually looking for chances to whinge about that animal Parker hurling my sandwiches into the Art room clay bin, or Lucy Prescott stalking me down corridors. But, if I wanted to, I could.

But I couldn't tell them this. Each time I geared myself up, I'd get some horror-show vision in my head of how they might take it. You only need half an ear hanging off one side of your head to know how some parents react. Flora knows someone whose mum wailed on for weeks about it all being *her* fault, then threw herself under a bus. That's something nice for Flora's friend to think about all her life. George has a neighbour whose son was banished. Banished! It sounds medieval, but it happened only last year. And I just read a novel where the father got drunk and cut the little circle of his son's face out of every single family photograph, and dropped the whole lot down the pan. The poor boy pads along to the bathroom in the middle of the night, and finds a little whirlpool of his own unflushed faces staring up at him. Maybe the author made that story up. I certainly hope so.

And then there's Mick. We met on holiday last summer and mooched around together quite a bit. When his dad won the accumulator at the races, and Mick clapped him on the back, he made a flinchy little face and moved away. I bet a heap Mick wishes he'd kept his trap shut.

So you can see why I kept putting it off. But we couldn't go on for ever. I was sick of not being able to do the simplest things, like keep a proper diary, or snap at Grandpa when he makes remarks about the couple on the corner, or leave the books I'm reading lying about

And that's how I told them. With a book. Not quite the way you'd imagine, but it worked. Mum and I were in Readerama a few weeks ago, and she was desperate not to let me out of sight because I was carrying most of the shopping. She didn't trust me not to put it down. Mum's of the view that trailing half a step behind every single shopper in town is a villain just waiting to pounce on their Priceworthy carriers, and make off down some dark alley. 'Have you got all the bags? You're supposed to have *six*,' she says to me every two minutes, and I've known her have breakdowns just from my slipping one half empty carrier inside another without sending her warning letters in triplicate first. She drives me mad. And she has the nerve to claim she's not that keen on me, when we're in town together. But I still get dragged along, as unpaid porter, whenever Dad's not available. It's my brute strength she's after, not my advice on broccoli versus sweetcorn, or red versus green for the new lavatory brush holder or, as on this particular morning, which cookery book to buy for Aunty Sarah's birthday.

'Just take the cheapest,' I said. 'It's not as if she ever gets round to actually cooking anything out of them, after all. She just flicks through them and then does chicken and chips.'

'What if she has it already?'

'Give her the receipt. Then she can bring it back and choose another. That way, *she* gets to be the one whose arms stretch down to the floor.'

Mum took the hint. 'All right,' she said unwillingly. 'You can put down the shopping. But don't move away from it. Stay where you are.'

'So what am I supposed to do?'

'Browse,' said my mother. 'That's what people do in bookshops. Have a little browse.'

I browsed. I browsed a step or so to the left (Health Matters). I browsed a step or so to the right (Feminism). I browsed forward a couple of steps (Family and Society), and back a few steps (Cars and Mechanical). And all the time I swear to God I never let a soul get between me and the shopping bags.

Then I got uppity. I browsed a little further away, past Holiday Guides, and round the back of Stamp Collecting. I ended up opposite Food and Drink and, copping a major glower from Mum, who was still choosing which of the eight million cookery books on display Aunty Sarah wouldn't change first, I doubled back through Computers.

Fetching up back at Health Matters, where I'd begun.

That's when I saw it. *Telling Your Parents: A Teenager's Guide to Coming Out in the Family.* You'd think the fairies might have put it there for me. I didn't do what you'd expect – slip it out and have a quick read while she was busy comparing *Feasts of Malaysia* with *You and Your Wok*, then creep back a few days later to read the rest. No. I simply took it off the shelf and tucked it under my arm. Then I dribbled the shopping bags one by one over to Mum at Gluttons' Corner, and stood there growing a beard down to my feet until she'd chosen.

'Right!' she said finally. 'I think this one's nice. She can't complain about this one.'

She waited for me to point out that Aunty Sarah can complain about anything. But I had bigger fish to fry.

I trailed her to the pay desk.

'Here,' she said, taking out her switch card and putting *Winter Cookery: A Casserole Lover's Collection* down on the counter.

'Here,' I said, laying *Telling Your Parents: A Teenager's Guide to Coming Out in the Family* straight down on top of it.

'What's that?'

'A book.'

'What book?' she said, playing for time as if she couldn't read.

'This book,' I said to her firmly. 'This book here.'

'Take it away, Gregory!' Her voice had shot up in the stratosphere. She was positively squeaking. And the poor girl at the pay desk didn't know where to look. (Would I have done it if it had been a bloke on duty that morning? Don't ask. I'll never know.)

'I mean it, Gregory!' Her hand shot out. The book went sailing off the desk on to the floor. 'I'm not buying that for you!'

I felt so sorry for her. But still I picked it up again and put it down on top of *Winter Cookery*.

'No, Gregory! No!' She swiped it off again.

I picked it up. 'Come on, Mum.'

Snatching it from me, she hurled it on the table to the side. 'No! *No!*'

'Yes, Mum,' I said, picking it up a third time.

'Oh, no! Oh, no! Oh, God, Gregory!' She reached for the book, but this time the salesgirl dived forward at the same time, maybe to pitch in on my side, maybe to save the book from yet another battering. When their hands met, the book slid off again on to the floor, falling open at a section called 'Telling the Grandparents'.

'Oh, God!' she wailed. 'I can't believe this is happening!' And I knew from the way it came out that the first of a thousand battles was over. Mum at least believed me.

I've never felt so dreadful in my life. I wanted to say 'I'm sorry', but I was worried she'd misunderstand, and get me wrong about the way I feel. So I said nothing. I just stood there like a giant lump, watching my own mum crumple, thanks to me.

Staff training at Readerama must be brilliant. Not only can the sales force read upside-down, but they know what to do at sticky moments. Glancing at the name on Mum's card, the girl said gently, 'Mrs Fisher, would you like to come through to the back and sit down for a moment? I could make you some coffee.'

Good thing it was my mum I'd dumped the newsflash on, and not my dad. He'd have dissolved into a puddle of tears and sat there for a week, weeping into his teacup. Mum's made of sterner stuff. She's kept her chin up through some moments of high embarrassment while raising me, and though this must have been about the worst, she still proved equal to the strain.

'That's very nice of you,' she said, pulling her coat straight and clutching her handbag closer. 'Most kind and thoughtful. But I'll be all right.'

The girl gave me a look, and pointed to one of those little stool things they use for getting to the upper shelves. I fetched it over. 'At least sit down,' she said to Mum. 'Just for a moment.'

'Just while you ring up the books, then,' Mum said, collapsing.

'Books', not 'book'. Did you notice? I did. So did the girl.

'It won't take a moment,' she said. But then she made a point of taking her time, sliding the card through the machine the wrong way once or twice, and rooting underneath the counter for a different sized bag, to give my mum a few moments. She even came out from behind the pay desk with the slip, and brought it over for Mum to sign. Mum's hand was shaking, but the signature looked close enough.

'There,' said the girl, managing to make it sound like 'There, there . . . ' and making me vow I'll never in my life buy any book in any shop on the planet but Readerama.

Mum raised her head. 'Well, Gregory. We can't stay here all day. Better get home.'

And tell your dad, she might have added. But I wasn't quite so worried about that. Dad has a flaming temper but in the end he always buys Mum's line on everything. He wasn't going to like it. Well, who would? Like anyone else, he'd like his son to grow up and marry and have a couple of kids, and not be different in any way. But not because the only thing he cares about is my being 'normal'. More because he's quite sure that being different – especially this way – is going to make absolutely everything in my life a whole lot more difficult for me. Once he's convinced this is the only way I'm going to be, he'll get a grip. He wants me happy more than he wants me straight. I'm lucky there. Some people want you straight a whole lot more than they want you happy.

The bus ride home was pretty quiet (if you don't count Mum saying, 'Gregory, have you got all the bags?' two dozen times). Once or twice, she touched my hand, as if she were about to say something. But it was not till we were walking into our own street that she came out with it.

'Let's not say anything about all this just for the moment.'

I gave her a suspicious look. What was she thinking? I wasn't old enough to know my mind? That this was something I was trying on, like some new style, or haircut? Did she think I was temporarily unhinged? Under someone's spell? Totally mistaken?

'Just for the moment,' she repeated. 'Just till we're sure.'

No point in climbing out of a box if you're going to climb straight back in again. 'I am sure. I've been sure for years now.'

'Well, waiting a little longer before you tell your father won't hurt, then, will it?'

'Mum,' I said. 'Give me one good reason not to tell him now.'

She looked quite hunted. 'You know how upset he's going to be, and we can't have him saying anything in front of Granny and Grandpa.'

Whoah, there! I stopped in my tracks. 'And why not?'

She stopped as well. 'Gregory, you know perfectly well why not.'

I put down the shopping, all six bags of it. 'Mum, you can't pick and choose who I keep this secret from,' I told her. 'It's too important. That has to be *my* decision.'

'But what if your grandpa finds out?'

'It's not a matter of him "finding out",' I said. 'Somebody has to tell him. Otherwise I'll be back exactly where I was before, having to watch myself all the time.'

'Is that so terrible?'

'Yes, it is!' I snapped. 'And it won't stop there, either. Within a week or so, you and Dad will be trying to kid yourselves it was all just a horrible mistake. No, I'm sorry, Mum. I'm not going back and it isn't fair to ask me.'

'Fair?' she hissed, striding off down the street again. '*Fair?* And what about what's fair on the rest of us? You'll give your grandpa a heart attack!'

I'd got her there. 'Oh, I don't think so,' I said, picking up everything and trailing after her. 'Didn't he go ballistic when you told him that Ginny was pregnant by Wayne Foster? And Gran cried for *weeks*. They were so upset and furious, they didn't even go to the wedding. And now look at them! Gran spends her whole life tangled up in pink knitting wool, and Grandpa won't put the baby down. They're tough. They'll get over it.'

Mum strode on furiously. 'Don't kid yourself they're going to come to terms with this quite so easily!'

'I don't see why not,' I said sullenly. 'They've got used to my terrible hair. And my terrible clothes. And my terrible music. And my terrible friends. And my . . .'

'Gregory! This is a whole lot more important than any of those!'

'Yes!' I yelled back. 'It certainly is! And that's exactly why I can't go on pretending all the time – not at school, and on the team, and with girls, and at home, and at my Saturday jobs, and *everywhere*. There's got to be *somewhere* I can just be *me*.'

Perhaps I'd got through to her. Or perhaps it was because we'd practically reached our own gate. But, suddenly, she seemed to soften a little. 'But surely waiting a little is only sensible. What if you change your mind?'

If this had been a school debate, I'd have come back at her pretty sharpish on that one, saying something like, 'I don't recall you ever saying that you put off marrying Dad in case you found out later that you were lesbian.' But this is my mum, don't forget. If I'd said that, she would have slapped me so hard I'd have gone reeling into Mr Skelley's hedge. So I said nothing.

She peered in my face. 'Oh, Gregory. This is going to take a whole lot of getting used to, and I can tell you one thing. The worst isn't over.'

'It is for me,' I told her quite truthfully.

And what if I did mean the lying, the secrets, the worrying, the pretending? Give me a break! She thought I meant that telling her had been the hardest thing. And that was important to her, you could tell. Shocked and upset as she was, you could still see she took it as a compliment that she mattered most. She took it seriously, the same way she took my blotchy finger painting from nursery, and my cracked pottery jewellery pot from primary school, and my split, wobbly stock cube dispenser from secondary school Woodwork. Her mouth even twitched a little, as if, if she didn't have to go in there and help me through Round Two with Dad, she might even have given me the tiniest of encouraging smiles.

I pushed the gate open. 'Ready?' I said, the same way she always used to say it to me when I was starting at a new school or a new club.

'I suppose so,' she muttered, exactly the same way I must have said it to her so many times before.

On our way up the path, she suddenly stopped and hurled herself into one of my shopping bags. Scattering socks and lightbulbs, she dragged out *Telling Your Parents: A Teenager's Guide*, and hurried off round the side of the house.

I set off in pursuit. 'What are you doing?'

'Stuffing this in the dustbin.'

'What, my *book*?'

But it was already gone, deep under tea leaves and old carrot peelings.

'It's not *your* book,' she said, slamming the lid down over the horrid mess. 'It's my book. I'm the one who paid for it.' She brushed tea leaves off her hands and added bitterly, 'Though I can't think why. You seem to be managing perfectly well without it.'

'But why shove it in the dustbin?'

'Listen, young man,' she warned me dangerously. 'Don't push your luck. If you're planning on making me *live* the bloody book, I'll be damned if I'll *dust* it.'

I know when a job's done. I just picked up the shopping and followed her in to face more of the music.

Further reading

You are likely to enjoy almost any of Anne Fine's many novels for teenagers. Two with a family theme are *Goggle Eyes* (Puffin Books, 2000), about an unwelcome potential stepfather, and *The Granny Project* (Corgi Children's Books, 2006).

Family Values

by Richard Benson

> The Bensons had farmed in Yorkshire for as long as anyone in the family could remember. Everyone expected the eldest son to join his father and carry on the tradition. But Richard was different. Farming didn't come naturally to him . . .

'All tha's to do is keep it straight, and watch to see nowt gets caught up in t' tines,'[1] my dad said as he stood on the step of our big green John Deere 2140[2] giving me instructions, and I sat in the driver's seat trying to look confident. 'And don't look so worried, lad, there's nowt much can go wrong. Tha tries too hard, tha knows.'

It was a cool autumn half-term evening, and I was about to try hard to power harrow one of my dad's fields. The power harrow was a machine about the size of a double bed that was pulled by a tractor through ploughed soil to produce a finer tilth.[3] Although it could get jammed and damaged if you were unlucky enough to fetch up a buried piece of old abandoned machinery, it presented no challenges to most people capable of driving tractors, and was a typical job to give to a boy in his mid teens, like me. I felt good being trusted with it, and encouraged by my dad telling me that I worried too much. I eased up the clutch and set off up the edge of our field. With the machine rattling and banging behind me, I even felt a sort of cockiness.

However, after about ten seconds, I noticed the tractor bonnet pointing away from the hedge despite my attempts to rein it back with the steering wheel. After fifteen I became aware that I was going backwards, and after eighteen I heard a terrible wrenching over the top of the engine. I disengaged the power,

---

[1]**tines**   prongs on the harrow
[2]**John Deere 2140**   a make of tractor
[3]**tilth**   cultivated soil

'All tha's to do is keep it straight'.

and looked back and around to see what had happened. It was bad. Somehow I had caught up the hedgerow in the tines, and roughly ten yards of hawthorn bush, roots and all, had been pulled into the machine until it stuck fast. I got off the tractor and walked around the mess scratching my head as if I knew what I was doing, just in case anyone was watching. Then I got back in, turned off the engine, and went looking for my dad.

The power-harrowing accident confirmed what had long been suspected by everyone at Rose Farm, i.e. that my tendency to get things wrong was not really down to youth or inexperience or bad luck, but to a near-total lack of concentration, coordination and instinct. When it came to farm jobs, I was generally useless, a liability, a danger to the people, animals and buildings around me. I couldn't steer straight, couldn't keep my mind focused, couldn't even shoo a pig along without falling over or letting it run through my legs. Mal and Karl[4]

---

[4] **Mal and Karl** workers on the Bensons' farm

looked nervously at each other when I climbed behind the wheel of a tractor. My dad tried to gee me up, but that just made me feel guilty. Boys on some farms got beaten for ineptitude like mine . . .

My dad was patient, and tried to get me to rely on my instincts: 'Tha tries too hard'; 'Don't look so worried'. Mal told me not to fret and said, 'When all else fails, try brute force and ignorance' – but I didn't have any brute force. Karl said, 'Just *do* it and don't think about it' – but what comes first, believing you can do something, or being able to do it?

    I couldn't just do those things, and it was hard to explain the admiration and jealousy I had for those who could. Once at teatime my dad said that he had been talking to the headmaster of Sowthistle School, and the headmaster had described someone as being 'an educated type – not like you, Gordon, practical'. My dad said he felt as if the headmaster might be patronizing him, and I got angry and said that of course he wouldn't have been. I told my dad that he didn't know what it was like not being able to do things, and then felt bad because it probably made him feel worse.

    Guy,[5] meanwhile, was emerging as a sort of child prodigy. By the age of ten he had assembled his own rudimentary toolbox and was making useful things out of wood. By eleven he was reversing trailers with a one-handed nonchalance.[6] By twelve he was growing vegetables in a patch of the garden behind the barn, having constructed an elaborate netting system to keep hungry birds off his seeds. He didn't talk about it – he just came home from school, changed his clothes, and ambled out to thin out a row of onions or pull up some weeds. Even before he graduated to proper crops and tools at the age of about fourteen, he had come to regard school as an inconvenience to be got out of the way each day before getting back to the vegetables or tools.

---

[5]**Guy**   Richard's brother
[6]**nonchalance**   casualness

Occasionally, briefly, something would capture his interest and pull him up to a teacher's excited attention. While showing no interest whatsoever in the sport, he had a talent for rugby and played for the school team before giving up; despite an indifference to art, when invited to draw a mother-in-law's tongue plant[7] he became interested in its leaves and drew an intricately detailed picture for which the teacher awarded him an A, and then showed no further interest in the subject for the rest of his school career. It seemed to me that as he walked off into the world of animals and vegetables, the universe beyond slowly melted away.

The chief objects of his affection were cats. There were usually between fifteen and twenty living around the farm, sleeping near the boiler in the outhouse, but a new stray turned up when Guy was twelve, and they befriended each other. When Top Cat died, he took others, which followed him about and seemed to stand apart from the other cats. He picked them up and rubbed them against the side of his face and smiled. He said he respected the cats because they did not tie themselves to him. He liked how they came and went, and did not demand affection when he did not want to give it.

It wasn't long before Guy could be relied on to do most things better than me, and so I settled for the idiot jobs: torch-shiner while they worked on mending fences; gate-opener when they were moving pigs; maggot-scraper when they cleaned pens out; flint-picker in the fields while they ploughed and harrowed.

I had more in common with Helen,[8] who although she liked the pigs, seemed to live on a different plane altogether. She was an abstracted little girl, happiest playing alone in a small wooden hut in the garden, climbing on straw-stacks, and swinging in an old tyre suspended from a beam in the barn. Her favourite things

---

[7]**mother-in-law's tongue plant**   common house plant with long, sharp leaves
[8]**Helen**   Richard's sister

were animals and fairy tales, and she said frequently that she wished she had been born a dog. When she and I worked on the farm, it usually involved us being directed by Guy.

My dad must have wondered what was happening. He worked hard and the farm was doing well, but while on other farms the children were looking after the animals while their parents took holidays, or going to discussion groups and bringing home new ideas, I was becoming a village joke, Guy was bizarrely self-absorbed and Helen was becoming a vegetarian. 'One day we're stroking them and giving them names, and the next thing you know you're taking it in a bag to someone or eating it!' she complained regularly, after the point in her early teens when she connected the meat to the pigs down the yard. She tolerated chicken, beef and lamb for a few years more because she thought all meat other than pork was a delicacy, but by the time she was sixteen she had converted entirely to fish and vegetables. 'You wouldn't have dared not eat meat when there was rationing,' said my dad.

'No, but there isn't rationing any more,' said Helen. 'Far from it when it comes to pork in our house.'

When I began to get good marks at Kirksfield School, people came to regard my relationship with my family and the farm as a source of amusement. My mum told visiting relatives that if she could combine Guy's hands with my brain, she would have the perfect son . . .

I thought about writing my dad and mum a letter of apology, but couldn't think what I'd say. I wished I could find an obscure skill to redeem myself, and then I wondered if I could do something with the pigs. I liked working with them – I was just scared of doing something wrong when someone else was there. I tried to think of a small job I could do that might make people say, 'Oh, he's no good wi' t' machinery but he's grand wi' t' animals.'

The only thing I could come up with was looking after ill pigs in my school holidays. Sometimes they got ill and were put into pens on their own, and thinking that I might be able to help them, I began trying to nurse the sick pigs back to health. It was easy but time-consuming, i.e. ideal for me, and in some cases just helping them eat and drink would bring them back round. Sometimes I made a hay-bale pen for them in the barn and went to feed, water and bed them up while Guy and my dad and Karl did something more important.

No one ever did say, 'He's grand wi' t' animals', but the possibility always seemed to be there, and I thought I had got a chance for glory one spring when a sow in the midst of giving birth got a piglet trapped across her cervix. Dislodging the piglet in such cases is not difficult: all you have to do is get your arm inside, push your first two fingers into the cervix, and pull the piglet around so its head is pointing towards you. You just have to be comfortable with inserting your bare forearm into a sow's birth canal, and to have a hand which is not so wide at the knuckle that it makes the sow uncomfortable. My dad sent me to bring a bucket with warm water and soap. As the swollen sow lay moaning on the floor, and Karl and I watched, he rolled up the shirt sleeve over his right arm, soaped up, and tried, but his fingers would barely go in. Karl tried and got knuckle-deep, but the sow began twitching. I thought my time had come. I can't say I was excited about the idea of putting my arm in there, but I felt that a calm, manful approach would only enhance the shift in the way everyone regarded me. I rubbed soap on, kneeled down at a right angle to the sow's bottom, and under the four expectant eyes, inserted thumb and finger tips into the bright pink distended labia. My fingers seemed to be going in fine, but I felt a sort of tight tube of muscle squeezing them, and she groaned. My damned hands! They obviously looked less masculine than Karl's, but were still too wide because, as the relatives had informed me, I had inherited them from my grandad.

'Ah, well. Go and ask thy mam to call t' vet,' said my dad. 'See if he can come straight away.'

I must have looked quite upset because when I walked past Karl he told me not to get down over such a daft thing. This, however, made me feel even worse.

Further reading

Richard Benson's *The Farm* (Penguin Book Ltd, 2006) describes the hardships of farming today and the end of the family farm. You might find the DVD *Winter Tales* (Dd Home Entertainment, 2006) interesting too. It tells the story of Hannah Hauxwell's struggle to survive alone on a Dales farm.

She's Leaving Home
by the Beatles

> The Beatles' songs were inspired by many things, from a newspaper article about there being 4,000 holes in Blackburn, Lancashire (used in the lyrics of *A Day in the Life*), to a Victorian circus poster (*Being for the Benefit of Mr Kite*). Some of their songs are wild fantasy (*I Am the Walrus*), others are more personal songs about loved and lost ones (*Julia*). Many of the lyrics can stand on their own as poems, including this one about an unknown girl.

Wednesday morning at five o'clock as the day begins
Silently closing her bedroom door
Leaving the note that she hoped would say more
She goes downstairs to the kitchen clutching her handker-
    chief
Quietly turning the backdoor key
Stepping outside she is free.
She (We gave her most of our lives)
    is leaving (Sacrificed most of our lives)
        home (We gave her everything money could buy)
She's leaving home after living alone
For so many years. Bye, bye.
Father snores as his wife gets into her dressing gown
Picks up the letter that's lying there
Standing alone at the top of the stairs
She breaks down and cries to her husband
Daddy our baby's gone.
Why would she treat us so thoughtlessly
How could she do this to me?
She (We never thought of ourselves)
    is leaving (Never a thought for ourselves)
        home (We struggled hard all our lives to get by)
She's leaving home after living alone
For so many years. Bye, bye.

Friday morning at nine o'clock she is far away
Waiting to keep the appointment she made
Meeting a man from the motor trade.
She (What did we do that was wrong)
   is having (We didn't know it was wrong)
     fun (Fun is the one thing that money can't buy)
Something inside that was always denied
For so many years. Bye, Bye.
She's leaving home bye bye.

Further reading

Find out more about the Beatles on the Internet: listen to their songs or read their lyrics. There are many websites, including http://www.beatleslyricsarchive.com. John Lennon also published poetry: try *In His Own Write* (Simon & Schuster Ltd, 2000).

Romeo and Juliet
by William Shakespeare

> A boy and girl, from two families who hate each other bitterly, fall in love and marry in secret. But Juliet's parents, Lord and Lady Capulet, have other plans for their daughter. They have arranged her marriage to a rich nobleman, Paris. She is horrified, but unable to confess her love for Romeo, the family's sworn enemy.

Act 3 Scene 5

LADY CAPULET	But now I'll tell thee joyful tidings, girl.
JULIET	And joy comes well in such a needy time.
	What are they, beseech¹ your ladyship?
LADY CAPULET	Well, well, thou hast a careful father, child,
	One who, to put thee from thy heaviness,
	Hath sorted out a sudden day of joy,
	That thou expects not, nor I looked not for.
JULIET	Madam, in happy time, what day is that?
LADY CAPULET	Marry², my child, early next Thursday morn,
	The gallant, young, and noble gentleman,
	The County Paris, at Saint Peter's Church,
	Shall happily make thee there a joyful bride.
JULIET	Now by Saint Peter's Church and Peter too,
	He shall not make me there a joyful bride.
	I wonder at this haste, that I must wed
	Ere he that should be husband comes to woo.
	I pray you tell my lord and father, madam,
	I will not marry yet, and when I do, I swear
	It shall be Romeo, whom you know I hate,
	Rather than Paris. These are news indeed!
LADY CAPULET	Here comes your father, tell him so yourself;
	And see how he will take it at your hands.

---

¹**beseech** beg
²**Marry** an exclamation of surprise

Enter CAPULET *and* NURSE.

CAPULET When the sun sets, the earth doth drizzle dew,
But for the sunset of my brother's son
It rains downright.
How now, a conduit³, girl? What, still in tears?
Evermore show'ring? In one little body   *130*
Thou counterfeits⁴ a bark⁵ a sea, a wind:
For still thy eyes, which I may call the sea,
Do ebb and flow with tears; the bark thy body is,
Sailing in this salt flood; the winds, thy sighs,
Who, raging with thy tears and they with them,   *135*
Without a sudden calm, will overset
Thy tempest-tossèd body. How now, wife,
Have you delivered to her our decree?

LADY CAPULET Ay, sir, but she will none, she gives you thanks.
I would the fool were married to her grave.   *140*

CAPULET Soft, take me with you, take me with you, wife.
How, will she none? doth she not give us thanks?
Is she not proud? doth she not count her blest,
Unworthy as she is, that we have wrought
So worthy a gentleman to be her bride?   *145*

JULIET Not proud you have, but thankful that you have:
Proud can I never be of what I hate,
But thankful even for hate that is meant love.

CAPULET How how, how how, chopt-logic? What is this?
'Proud', and 'I thank you', and 'I thank you not',   *150*
And yet 'not proud', mistress minion you?
Thank me no thankings, nor proud me no
  prouds,
But fettle your fine joints 'gainst Thursday next,
To go with Paris to Saint Peter's Church,
Or I will drag thee on a hurdle thither.   *155*

---

³**conduit** a water spout
⁴**counterfeits** are like, imitate
⁵**bark** a small boat

104   Conflict and confusion

Disobedient wretch!

	Out, you green-sickness carrion! out, you baggage!
	You tallow-face!
LADY CAPULET	Fie, fie, what, are you mad?
JULIET	Good father, I beseech you on my knees,
	Hear me with patience but to speak a word.
	[She kneels down.]

CAPULET	Hang thee, young baggage, disobedient wretch!	160
	I tell thee what: get thee to church a' Thursday,	
	Or never after look me in the face.	
	Speak not, reply not, do not answer me!	
	My fingers itch. Wife, we scarce thought us blest	
	That God had lent us but this only child,	165
	But now I see this one is one too much,	
	And that we have a curse in having her.	
	Out on her, hilding!⁶	
NURSE	God in heaven bless her!	
	You are to blame, my lord, to rate her so.	
CAPULET	And why, my Lady Wisdom? Hold your tongue,	170
	Good Prudence, smatter with your gossips, go.	
NURSE	I speak no treason.	
CAPULET	O God-i-goden!⁷	
NURSE	May not one speak?	
CAPULET	Peace, you mumbling fool!	
	Utter your gravity o'er a gossip's bowl,	
	For here we need it not.	
LADY CAPULET	You are too hot.	175
CAPULET	God's bread, it makes me mad! Day, night, work, play,	
	Alone, in company, still my care hath been	
	To have her matched; and having now provided	
	A gentleman of noble parentage,	
	Of fair demesnes,⁸ youthful and nobly ligned,	180
	Stuffed, as they say, with honourable parts,	
	Proportioned as one's thought would wish a man,	
	And then to have a wretched puling fool,	
	A whining mammet, in her fortune's tender,⁹	

---

⁶**hilding** wretch
⁷**God-i-goden** good evening
⁸**demesnes** land, estate
⁹**tender** offer

	To answer 'I'll not wed, I cannot love; *185*

        To answer 'I'll not wed, I cannot love;   *185*
        I am too young, I pray you pardon me.'
        But and you will not wed, I'll pardon you:
        Graze where you will, you shall not house with
           me.
        Look to't, think on't, I do not use to jest.
        Thursday is near, lay hand on heart, advise: *190*
        And you be mine, I'll give you to my friend;
        And you be not, hang, beg, starve, die in the
           streets,
        For by my soul, I'll ne'er acknowledge thee,
        Nor what is mine shall never do thee good.
        Trust to't, bethink you, I'll not be forsworn.   *195*
        Exit CAPULET
JULIET   Is there no pity sitting in the clouds
        That sees into the bottom of my grief?
        O sweet my mother, cast me not away!
        Delay this marriage for a month, a week,
        Or if you do not, make the bridal bed   *200*
        In that dim monument where Tybalt lies.
LADY CAPULET   Talk not to me, for I'll not speak a word.
        Do as thou wilt, for I have done with thee.
        Exit LADY CAPULET

Further reading

In the 1990s, the BBC broadcast animations of 12 of Shakespeare's plays, which had been abridged and adapted by Leon Garfield. All 12, including *Romeo and Juliet*, are now available on the DVD *Shakespeare's Animated Tales* (Metrodome Distribution, 2005). There are also plenty of retellings, many of them using Shakespeare's own words, such as Marcia Williams' amusingly illustrated *Tales from Shakespeare* (Candlewick Press, 2004).

Activities

Buried Treasure

Before you read

For questions 1 and 2, discuss your ideas in a small group, making notes if you wish, then share your thoughts with the rest of your class.

1. Would you like to be part of a big family? What are some of the advantages and disadvantages?

2. What do you know about family life in the 1940s? What would you imagine to be some of the biggest differences from family life today?

What's it about?

Read the story and answer question 3 by yourself. Then compare your answer with a partner's.

3. The story is set in 1946, at the end of World War II. What period details can you find? What aspects of family life haven't changed? Make notes to exchange with a partner.

Thinking about the text

4. Working with a partner, improvise a scene in which Tom talks to a friend, telling the story of his accident and describing his sister. Think about:
   - his excuses for tormenting his sister
   - what he thinks about Polly
   - how he feels when she hugs him.

5. On page 57, Polly says: 'Feelings were so muddled'. Write two paragraphs describing the different feelings Polly has for Rachel and Tom. How does she show these 'muddled feelings' through what she says and does? Quote from the text to support your opinions.

6. Write a short character sketch of Rachel and Polly. What are the main differences between them? Who do you find most sympathetic? Why?

7. Working in a group, try turning the story into a short play. Think about:
   - how many scenes you will need
   - how to set out a drama script (names in the margin, no speech marks, stage directions in brackets)
   - how you will convey Polly's inner thoughts and feelings.

A Parents' and Teenagers' Alphabet Book and *Urgent Note to My Parents*

Before you read

1 What kind of poetry do you like best? Poems about feelings, humorous poems, poems that rhyme, or poems which tell a story? Or some other kind? Discuss your preferences in a small group.

What's it about?

Read the two poems and answer questions 2 and 3 by yourself. Then compare your answers with a partner's.

2 **a** Who is being described in the first poem? (The title is a clue.) Why does the poet include the instruction 'delete to taste'?
  b Who is speaking in the second poem?
  c Take it in turns to read the poems aloud with your partner. What tone of voice will you use for each poem?

3 There is no punctuation in the long note at the end of the first poem. Write a short paragraph explaining why you think that is, and what effect it has.

Thinking about the text

4 **a** What do the following figures of speech mean?
  - *driving up the wall*
  - *getting on a high horse*
  - *laying down the law*
  - *pointing the finger*
  - *a bone to pick*

  b Make a list of figures of speech that describe family arguments; for example, 'losing your rag', or 'blowing a gasket'.

5 Look carefully at the pattern of the alphabet poem. Use it as a model for your own Parents' and Teenagers', or Brothers' and Sisters', Alphabet Book.

6 Do you sympathise with the writer of *Urgent Note to My Parents*? As a teenager, are there times when you feel you are asked to be 'where I can't be?' Draw two columns headed 'Old enough' and 'Not old enough', and then fill in some examples (e.g. 'old enough to tidy my room', 'not old enough to stay out late').

One Small Step

Before you read

1 Working in a small group, try to summarise some of the main contrasts between Eastern and Western family expectations. In what ways do you think life for an Asian in Britain would have been different in the 1960s?

2 Do you have family arguments about what you wear, or how you spend your leisure time? What lies behind your parents' objections? Discuss your ideas in a small group.

What's it about?

Read the story and answer questions 3 to 5 by yourself. Then discuss your ideas in a small group.

3 The story is full of 'period detail' describing life in the 1960s. Find three details in the text which strike you as the most different from life today. Compare your list with your partner's – have you chosen the same three?

4 What are the main differences between Mala's and her mother's experience of being an immigrant?

5 What do Mala and her friends find so exciting about the first walk on the moon? How does this event link to Mala's own life, and to the title of the story?

Thinking about the text

6 Think about the language the writer uses to tell this story, particularly the dialogue. What particular words and phrases help you to imagine the different characters and hear their voices? Write a paragraph or two explaining your choices.

7 Mala says: 'there was a new voice in my head that questioned everything Ma believed in.' Working in a pair, improvise a scene between Mala and her mother in which they argue about Mala's friends.

8 Towards the end of the story (pages 75–6), the writer describes some of the lessons Mala learned as she entered the adult world. Imagine that you are Mala, grown-up: write a letter to your mother apologising for being such a difficult daughter.

Independence

Before you read

1 What would you find hardest if you were imprisoned or in hiding? Think about the things you would miss as well as the physical hardship. Discuss your ideas with a partner.

2 People keep diaries for different reasons; for example, to express their private feelings, or to record events. Have you ever kept one yourself? What kind of diary would you find most useful? Discuss your ideas with a partner.

What's it about?

3 In a small group, discuss the kind of person you imagine Anne to be. Do you think she would have been exceptional whatever her life had been like?

Thinking about the text

4 Do you think Anne is right when she says 'I don't need the support of Mother or anyone else'? What might you miss if you no longer lived with your parents or carers? Discuss your ideas in a small group, then report back to the rest of your class.

5 Anne writes of Peter: 'I'm not alone any more. He loves me'. What difference did their situation make to Anne and Peter's relationship? Why do you imagine Anne's father worried about it? Write a letter from him to his daughter, explaining his point of view.

6 Anne writes: 'I *will* improve myself.' Write another imaginary entry for Anne's diary, describing how she tries to make amends. Try to match your language to the original; for example, follow her use of exclamation marks, her expressiveness and her lively tone of voice.

Getting the Messages

Before you read

1 What kind of issues would you find it hard to discuss with your parents? Share your thoughts in a small group.

What's it about?

Read the story and answer questions 2 to 4 by yourself. Then compare your answers with a partner's.

2 What makes the hero put off telling his parents? What finally changes his mind? Quote from the text to back up your opinion.

3 What evidence in the text can you find that suggests the boy and his mother have a close relationship?

4 The boy and his mother experience a range of feelings during the course of the story. Draw a graph to show their ups and downs, labelling them to explain the causes.

Thinking about the text

5 'And that's how I told them. With a book.' How else might Gregory have broken the news? Why do you think he chose to do it that way? Was he right? With a partner, discuss alternatives that might have been less embarrassing for his mother.

6 How do you imagine the boy and his mother will tell the rest of the family? Improvise the scene.

7 How does Anne Fine build tension through the story? For instance, find examples of:
- keeping information from the reader
- sentence length
- use of humour
- exaggeration.

Make a list, then discuss it with a partner.

Family Values

Before you read

1 Do you know what expectations your family has of you? Do they match your own expectations? Are they realistic? In what ways if any do you feel different from your family? Discuss your ideas in a small group.

What's it about?

Read the text and answer questions 2 and 3 by yourself. Then compare your answers with a partner's.

2 Sum up the 'family values' that Richard couldn't share. In what ways was he different?

3 What made Richard a 'liability' for everyone around him?

Thinking about the text

4 Can you think of a time when you found it particularly difficult to master a new skill – perhaps learning to swim, or speaking a foreign language, or making something? What were your feelings? Were others sympathetic? How did you handle your failure? Write about your experience.

5 At one point, Richard considers writing a letter of apology to his parents. What might he have said? Write the letter he never sent.

6 A review described *The Farm* as 'easy and relaxed in tone, spiced with humorous incidents and amusingly blunt dialogue'. Find examples of the different features mentioned. What effect do the words and phrases you have chosen have on the reader? Do you agree with the reviewer? Write a short review of your own. Is there anything else you might mention?

She's Leaving Home

Before you read

1 What do you know already about the Beatles? Find out about the way they worked together – for instance, did words or music come first when they were writing a song, and did they compose together or separately?

What's it about?

2 Read the lyric by yourself, and then make a list of questions for your partner. For example:
   - Who is speaking in the bracketed sentences?
   - Where is the girl going?

   Have clear ideas about what the answers might be. Then swap lists, answer your partner's questions, and discuss your ideas.

3 Are there any details that suggest this is a song lyric rather than a poem?

4 Make a list of all the things the parents did for their daughter, referring directly to the text.

Thinking about the text

5 Parents frequently complain that they gave their child 'everything money could buy'. What are your views about this? Is it true that 'Fun is the one thing that money can't buy'? Hold a class debate. You will need two speakers for and two against the motion ('Money can't buy fun') and you should make notes of all the main points before you begin, so that you can argue clearly.

6 Imagine you are the girl who's leaving home. Write the letter that you leave for your parents. Look for clues in the lyric which help to explain the relationship with her parents. Try to explain your reasons for going.

7 We get only a brief snapshot of the girl and her parents and we don't know what happens next. For instance, is the 'man from the motor trade' in love with her or will he dump her? Will she come home or has she gone for good? Decide what might happen and then, in a small group, improvise their next meeting.

Romeo and Juliet

Before you read

1 What do you know already about the story of Romeo and Juliet? What other Shakespeare plays have you read or seen? How do you feel about his work? What have you enjoyed or disliked? Discuss your ideas in a small group.

What's it about?

2 Read the scene in a group of four, taking a part each. Note any words or phrases that puzzle you. Read it again, taking different parts. Then try to put it into your own words.

3 In a small group, discuss why Juliet is crying at the beginning of the scene. What does her father think she's crying about? What does he threaten to do if Juliet disobeys him?

4 Make a list of words and phrases that convey Juliet's parents' anger. How do the phrases differ from today's language?

Thinking about the story

5 Work in a small group. Put Juliet's father in the hot seat. The rest of the group should question him and try to explain Juliet's feelings. Juliet's father should present his points as fairly as possible.

6 In Shakespeare's day, arranged marriages were more common than they are today. Discuss your own views on this subject with a partner.

7 Look closely at the vocabulary, sentence structure and punctuation in this extract. In what ways do they differ from modern speech? Refer to examples in the text to illustrate your comments. Then have a go at translating Capulet's speech beginning 'God's bread' (page 105) into modern English.

Compare and contrast

1 Working in a small group, devise a television programme about conflict between parents and teenagers. One of you should be the presenter, and the others should play characters from the extracts. Think about the sort of questions the presenter might ask, and the sort of answers the characters might give. You could prepare a script, or perform the programme as an improvisation.

2 Choose three texts from this section. Make brief notes about the different aspects of family conflict that are represented in them. Use your notes to write an essay evaluating how successful the writers are in conveying what it is like to be a teenager. What writing techniques do they use to achieve their effects? Which is your favourite of the three pieces, and why?

3 Imagine that the mothers from *One Small Step* and *Getting the Messages* could meet. What might they say to each other about their 'difficult' children? What might they agree about? Write a short playscript, or work on an improvisation with a small group.

4 In their very different ways, *She's Leaving Home* and *Romeo and Juliet* both deal with daughters who rebel. Their parents show some similar reactions. Write a short essay pointing out significant similarities and differences in style, mood and content. Among other things you could think about:
- differences between dramatic and lyric forms
- the settings
- contrasts between contemporary and Elizabethan language
- the attitudes of the parents.

3 Change and uncertainty

I'm not in that picture.

The pieces in this section all deal with the upheaval that change can bring to families. There are many different reasons for family breakdown or separation. Sometimes it is caused by outside events, such as war or emigration, where families may lose their identity and be forced to adapt to a new environment.

Many children in families today cope with complex relationships caused by divorce and remarriage. They find themselves juggling their lives between two separate homes, or learning to accept new brothers and sisters. Perhaps you or your friends have first-hand experience of this. Step-families can lead to conflicting loyalties, and there are no easy solutions.

There doesn't always have to be a dramatic reason, such as emigration or divorce, for family upheaval. Sometimes the change and uncertainty is the result of children growing up and leading independent lives.

Activities

Discuss the following questions in a small group.

1 What novels, plays or short stories have you read which tackle this subject? Which ones gave you the clearest sense of the characters' predicament? How did the writer achieve this? Have you seen any films or television programmes about family breakdown? Which ones stayed in your mind, and why?

2 Not all aspects of change are negative. What are some of the advantages, say, of having two families?

3 Can you think of an example in the news recently where families were disrupted by war or famine? What happened to them? What would you find hardest in these situations?

Lost and Found

by Rachel Anderson

> Rachel Anderson is a previous winner of the *Guardian* Children's Fiction Award. She has written several novels with war settings, including *Warlands* (Oxford University Press, 2001), the story of a Vietnamese orphan born amongst the bombings and terrors of war. In this text she describes her own adoption of a child, which gave her writing a special insight into war orphans' troubled lives.

In a flowery city in a faraway country, a baby was lying in a gutter. He was dirty, covered in sores, and so thin that his rib-bones pushed against his skin. He was hungry. He'd nearly stopped bothering to cry. Nobody took any notice of him. Babies were often abandoned on the street. Older children lived in cardboard boxes, and scratched about on rubbish dumps like chickens.

The night was noisy with bombs being dropped onto the villages outside the city. People were hurrying to get home before the curfew. A policeman on a bicycle heard the baby whimper. He picked the little boy up, took him to the nearest orphanage. It was called *Hoi Duc Anh*, which means 'Society for the Protection of Infants'. He left him in the office on a wicker chair.

Later, the boy-baby was wrapped in a piece of cloth for a nappy and laid in a cot. He stayed there, day and night, for several years. Twice a day he was fed. Once a day he was carried outside to the yard and hosed with water alongside the other unwanted babies, toddlers and children. As he grew up into a boy, he had a mat on the floor.

Some days, mothers or aunties or grannies came to the Hoi Duc Anh looking for their lost children. But in six years, nobody came looking for this child. He was given the name Nguyen Thanh Sang. Nobody knows now who gave it to him. Perhaps one of the women who worked in the orphanage.

Nguyen Thanh Sang had no toys, no books, no television, no chocolate, no aunties visiting, no school to go to. He smiled but he didn't learn to speak. One day when he was about five or six, some of the orphanage helpers gave him a red wooden brick and tried to teach him to walk.

When the fighting and the bombing was nearly over, Nguyen Thanh Sang was taken on a bus with 99 other children that nobody could agree what to do with. They loaded them onto a plane to Kuala Lumpur[1] where the plane re-fuelled, then flew on to Britain. Nobody wanted them here either, except for the youngest, if they were pretty, and girls.

Most of the children had lots of disabilities. Nguyen Thanh Sang couldn't hear very well because of the bombs. He couldn't walk very well because of lying in a cot for so long, and not having had enough to eat, and he couldn't speak, but he grinned at anybody who looked at him. This was scary because he had so many black and missing teeth.

Nobody ever asked him what he wanted. He was taken with 19 other children from the faraway city to another orphanage. He stayed there for five years. Then, one Sunday in Spring, I met him. And he came to live with me. He called me Mum. I called him Sang. I am still his mum. He is still my son, Sang.

Nobody came looking for this child.

---

[1]**Kuala Lumpur**   capital city of Malaysia

Sang is now a grown-up man. But inside sometimes, he is still a frightened, confused, lost boy that nobody knew what to do with. Most of the time, however, he is happy. On Mondays, he plays five-a-side football. On Saturdays, he works in a café next to a cathedral and makes sandwiches and serves tea to visitors. Twice a year, he goes to the Blood Donation Centre and gives some of his blood to be used for sick people.

Nobody knows his real birth date, not even what year he was born. But we do know the date that he came to live in my family. So, on the 21st anniversary of that date, we had a big celebration. Lot of food, cakes, fizzy drinks, champagne, laughing and music. People brought him cards and presents. People sang to him, and cheered him.

When the speeches and praises were over, Sang himself said in a quiet voice, 'I make a speech too.'

He is shy, can't always remember numbers or words, and can't talk clearly. But he stood up in front of a big crowd of friends and relations, and this is what he said: 'Thank you for coming to this party. I am glad you came. I like the presents you bring me. I like my family here. And now one thing. I am thinking about the other children who come on the plane from Vietnam with me to this country. And I want us all to think about them. Some of them still quite sad, in children's home. One of them, Kim Yen, she has died. The others, some of them still there. We'll think of them.'

Then he began to weep. And his big sister wept with him. And they held each other tight in their arms. And some of the rest of us wept too.

Sang's nephew, who is called Nguyen after his uncle's first name, said, 'Why are all the grown-ups crying?'

I said, 'We're crying because we're so happy and proud that Uncle Sang is here and always reminds us to think about other people too.'

The next day, a visitor to the café where Sang works, said to him. 'What a lucky young lad you are to have found such a big family to adopt you!'

Lucky? Losing everything in the world, including his own country? No, we're the lucky ones, to have him here in the middle of our family.

Further reading

If you have enjoyed reading about Sang, you might like some of Rachel Anderson's other novels as well. Try *Red Moon* (Hodder Children's Books, 2006), or visit her website (http://www.rachelanderson.co.uk) for a list of all her books.

A Family Photo
by Lynette Craig

> This and the following three pieces share one theme, although they approach it differently. This poem is written from a child's viewpoint.

This is my dad,
That's my step-mum, Irene,
And this is the baby, Annie.
That's their dog, Dozer,
He's so funny,
He always sits under the table.

No, I'm not in that picture.

Further reading

If you liked this poem, you might enjoy Craig's poetry collection *Burning Palaces* (Flarestack Publishing, 2006).

Two of Everything
by Jackie Kay

> Like *A Family Photo*, this poem is written from a child's perspective, but this poem focuses on duplication rather than absence – or does it?

My friend Shola said to me that she said to her mum:
'It's not fair, Carla (that's me) has two of everything:

Carla has two bedrooms,
two sets of toys, two telephones,

two wardrobes, two door mats,
two mummies, two cats,

two water purifiers, two kitchens,
two environmentally friendly squeezies.'

My friend Shola said to me that she said to her mum:
'Why can't you and Dad get divorced?'

But the thing Shola doesn't even realize yet,
is that there are two of me.

Further reading

Jackie Kay has published several collections of poetry, including *Two's Company* (Puffin Books, 1992), and an autobiographical novel, *Strawgirl* (Macmillan Children's Books, 2003), about a black girl's adoption by a white Scottish couple.

Saturday Fathers
by Kit and the Widow

> This lyric looks at family breakdown from a different viewpoint – the fathers'.

Here's to the Saturday fathers
You see at MacDonalds and such,
The ones that are not above bribery
Spoiling that little too much;
The ones in the queue for the movie
Nobody's desperate to see;
Here's to the Saturday fathers,
Glamorous and generous and free.

Here's to the Saturday fathers
Wearing that air of disgrace,
Pushing the swings at the playground
From behind so you don't see their face.
Not talking much about Granny,
Sweaty in yesterday's shirt,
Here's to the Saturday fathers,
Clumsy and helpless and hurt.

Here's to the Saturday fathers
Hearing about friends they can't meet,
Whose one single dread is the silence,
The boredom that signals defeat.
Handing them back on the doorstep,
Here's to the toneless exchange,
Here's to the Saturday fathers,
Remote and unsettling and strange.

Here's to the Saturday fathers
Not the daddy they have in the week;

The six o'clock hugs which are laden
With feelings too frantic to speak.
The dads who must make do with courtesy
And if they want more, then that's tough.
Here's to the Saturday fathers
Punished far more than enough.

Further reading

Kit and the Widow are a double act, performing humorous songs. They have published a double CD album, *Les Enfants du Parody* (The Classical Recording Company, 2001), and, more recently, the CD *100 Not Out* (The Classical Recording Company, 2007).

New Families: the Experience of Divorce

> In this extract from *Parent Problems!* (edited by Bren Neale and Amanda Wade; Young Voice, 2000) a group of children and young people share their experiences of life after parents split up.

Selina (16)
Having two homes is like putting your life into a couple of carrier bags every week.

Beth (14)
If you're constantly moving from one house to the other you feel a bit sort of lonely and stuff – if you're in one of those neighbourhoods where it's like not the done thing. Dad's keen on me inviting friends over to his house, but it's got a strange smell and I get a bit worried that people will notice and think, 'Oh those deprived people living in a place that's falling to pieces' and they won't want to go there.

Tom (12)
We have to send out a search party when toys get lost. There's a kind of Bermuda Triangle in the middle of the houses where toys just seem to disappear.

Becky (13)
I don't like the food at dad's, how they cook and that. They shop at SuperFare and it's disgusting. And there's always dog hairs in it 'cos we've got two dogs. So I don't really eat much there, I just say I'm full.

Fred (10)
The only drawback is that we forget things we want – like toys and music stuff. It takes a lot of doing, getting it from the other house.

Claudia (12)
I'd prefer it if mum and dad lived closer because it's a hassle if I forget my school books and I can't leave them in my school locker 'cos it's full of smelly PE kit.

Rachel (16)
I find that I'm a different person at each house – the way I behave changes, 'cos of the different atmospheres and 'cos at dad's there's a new partner around and 'cos my parents react differently to things. So I adapt to my environment, I suppose. Like I study more at my dad's and watch TV more here – 'cos there's little kids about here.

Bob (12)
About a year ago I would come home from a weekend with dad, and find it very hard to re-adjust – sometimes it's just too much. Mum was always very understanding and I used to have a lot of Mondays off school and then by the Tuesday I'd be fine.

Matt (14)
It's just a drag really, for me, swapping over every other day. Just not being able to settle down in one place for longer than one night. It's just my room. Really it doesn't feel ever lived in as it would if I was at one house all the time.

Rachel (16)
Change-over time is a bit weird. You've got to settle in. Because you sort of change, depending what house you're at.

Tom (12)
There's still the problem that's impossible to solve, that we don't see both parents all the time as we used to.

Selina (16)
I'd really love not to have to move house every week. It's not about mum and dad being together – that's not the important thing. It's about me and my brother not having a permanent base.

Caroline (17)
It didn't work for me having two bases because you've got like two bedrooms and two of everything and I was getting mixed up who I was.

Lisa (8)
It isn't difficult for me. You walk in at dad's, you think, 'Ah, late night tonight, stories, cornetto' and at mum's you think, 'Ah, nice early night tonight, nice little bowl of cereal and some lovely hot chocolate.'

Nina (11)
My family is pretty ordinary except that we don't see our dad that much. Most of my friends' families are split up, except it's not as formal as that 'cos mum and dad still see each other a lot. He comes over three or four times a week. Seeing dad is just like, normal. It's not like a special visit or anything. I sometimes call in at his place but I don't stay. I'd get a bit bored, 'cos he hasn't got a TV.

Maya (14)
I live with my mum, step dad, and little sister. I can't remember my real dad. He's not part of my family.

Joseph (9)
I've always lived in a different place from my dad. He lives 200 miles away and I stay with him six times a year. He comes down once a month for the weekend and takes me to a hotel. My grandparents are very close. My mum works, so I stop off at gran's after school and I sometimes sleep over there. Home is basically all their houses.

Maria (13)
I live with my mum and sister. I don't really see much of my dad. I see him when he turns up.

Catherine (20)
Home was with my mum because the only time I ever saw my dad was at Christmas. But I see more of him now.

Sally (12)
My family is my brother, step dad, half brother, mum and dad and my dad's fiancée. I've got two homes. My dad, brother and I live here, and my mum's side live fifteen miles away. Every Tuesday mum picks me up at five o'clock and then brings me back at eight, and I go every other weekend.

Claudia (12)
If you didn't love your mum or you didn't love your dad, then, by law, you'd be a family but you wouldn't really feel like a family. 'Cos, I mean, it doesn't matter if you're rich or poor, as long as you love each other. Of course, you're going to have arguments and stuff, but if you love each other it doesn't matter really, does it, what sort of family you're in?

Further reading

Parent Problems! is one of a series of books published by Young Voice, a charity 'dedicated to making young people's view heard'. If you want to know more, the book contains a list of useful resources and contacts, including helplines; or you can visit the website at http://www.whenparentspart.org.uk.

You might also enjoy Anne Fine's novel *Step by Wicked Step* (Yearling Books, 1997), in which a group of teenagers tell their personal stories about 'new' families.

The Ultimate Safari

by Nadine Gordimer

> Nadine Gordimer is a celebrated white South African novelist and short story writer, who received the Nobel Prize for Literature in 1991. Most of her works deal with the tensions of her racially divided home country. She has experienced at first hand the dire effects of war on families caught up in it. Her father was a refugee, like the characters in this story, although he had to flee from Tsarist Russia, not Mozambique.

That night our mother went to the shop and she didn't come back. Ever. What happened? I don't know. My father also had gone away one day and never come back; but he was fighting in the war. We were in the war, too, but we were children, we were like our grandmother and grandfather, we didn't have guns. The people my father was fighting – the bandits,[1] they are called by our government – ran all over the place and we ran away from them like chickens chased by dogs. We didn't know where to go. Our mother went to the shop because someone said you could get some oil for cooking. We were happy because we hadn't tasted oil for a long time; perhaps she got the oil and someone knocked her down in the dark and took that oil from her. Perhaps she met the bandits. If you meet them, they will kill you. Twice they came to our village and we ran and hid in the bush and when they'd gone we came back and found they had taken everything; but the third time they came back there was nothing to take, no oil, no food, so they burned the thatch and the roofs of our houses fell in. My mother found some pieces of tin and we put those up over part of the house. We were waiting there for her that night she never came back.

We were frightened to go out, even to do our business, because the bandits did come. Not into our house – without a

---

[1] **bandits** gangs of robbers

roof it must have looked as if there was no one in it, everything gone – but all through the village. We heard people screaming and running. We were afraid even to run, without our mother to tell us where. I am the middle one, the girl, and my little brother clung against my stomach with his arms round my neck and his legs round my waist like a baby monkey to its mother. All night my first-born brother kept in his hand a broken piece of wood from one of our burnt house-poles. It was to save himself if the bandits found him.

We stayed there all day. Waiting for her. I don't know what day it was; there was no school, no church any more in our village, so you didn't know whether it was a Sunday or a Monday.

When the sun was going down, our grandmother and grandfather came. Someone from our village had told them we children were alone, our mother had not come back. I say 'grandmother' before 'grandfather' because it's like that: our grandmother is big and strong, not yet old, and our grandfather is small, you don't know where he is, in his loose trousers, he smiles but he hasn't heard what you're saying, and his hair looks as if he's left it full of soap suds. Our grandmother took us – me, the baby, my first-born brother, our grandfather – back to her house and we were all afraid (except the baby, asleep on our grandmother's back) of meeting the bandits on the way. We waited a long time at our grandmother's place. Perhaps it was a month. We were hungry. Our mother never came. While we were waiting for her to fetch us our grandmother had no food for us, no food for our grandfather and herself. A woman with milk in her breasts gave us some for my little brother, although at our house he used to eat porridge, same as we did. Our grandmother took us to look for wild spinach but everyone else in her village did the same and there wasn't a leaf left.

Our grandfather, walking a little behind some young men, went to look for our mother but didn't find her. Our grandmother cried with other women and I sang the hymns with them. They brought a little food – some beans – but after two days there was nothing again. Our grandfather used to have three sheep and a cow and a vegetable garden but the bandits had long ago taken the sheep and the cow, because they were hungry, too; and when planting time came our grandfather had no seed to plant.

So they decided – our grandmother did; our grandfather made little noises and rocked from side to side, but she took no notice – we would go away. We children were pleased. We wanted to go away from where our mother wasn't and where we were hungry. We wanted to go where there were no bandits and there was food. We were glad to think there must be such a place; away.

Our grandmother gave her church clothes to someone in exchange for some dried mealies[2] and she boiled them and tied them in a rag. We took them with us when we went and she thought we would get water from the rivers but we didn't come to any river and we got so thirsty we had to turn back. Not all the way to our grandparents' place but to a village where there was a pump. She opened the basket where she carried some clothes and the mealies and she sold her shoes to buy a big plastic container for water. I said, *Gogo*, how will you go to church now even without shoes, but she said we had a long journey and too much to carry. At that village we met other people who were also going away. We joined them because they seemed to know where that was better than we did.

To get there we had to go through the Kruger Park. We knew about the Kruger Park. A kind of whole country of animals – elephants, lions, jackals, hyenas, hippos, crocodiles, all kinds of animals. We had some of them in our own country, before the war (our grandfather remembers; we children weren't born yet) but the bandits kill the elephants and sell their tusks, and the bandits and our soldiers have eaten all the buck. There was a man in our village without legs – a crocodile took them off, in our river; but all the same our country is a country of people, not animals. We knew about the Kruger Park because some

---

[2]**mealies**   ears of sweetcorn, maize

of our men used to leave home to work there in the places where white people come to stay and look at the animals.

So we started to go away again. There were women and other children like me who had to carry the small ones on their backs when the women got tired. A man led us into the Kruger Park; are we there yet, are we there yet, I kept asking our grandmother. Not yet, the man said, when she asked him for me. He told us we had to take a long way to get round the fence, which he explained would kill you, roast off your skin the moment you touched it, like the wires high up on poles that give electric light in our towns. I've seen that sign of a head without eyes or skin or hair on an iron box at the mission hospital[3] we used to have before it was blown up.

When I asked the next time, they said we'd been walking in the Kruger Park for an hour. But it looked just like the bush we'd been walking through all day, and we hadn't seen any animals except the monkeys and birds which live around us at home, and a tortoise that, of course, couldn't get away from us. My first-born brother and the other boys brought it to the man so it could be killed and we could cook and eat it. He let it go because he told us we could not make a fire; all the time we were in the Park we must not make a fire because the smoke would show we were there. Police, wardens, would come and send us back where we came from. He said we must move like animals among the animals, away from the roads, away from the white people's camps. And at that moment I heard – I'm sure I was the first to hear – cracking branches and the sound of something parting grasses and I almost squealed becaue I thought it was the police, wardens – the people he was telling us to look out for – who had found us already. And it was an elephant, and another elephant, and more elephants, big blots of dark moved wherever you looked between the trees . . .

---

[3] **mission hospital**   hospital run by religious missionaries, often Christians, who go to a foreign country to do charitable work and spread word of their religion

We walked at night as well as by day. We could see the fires where the white people were cooking in the camps and we could smell the smoke and the meat. We watched the hyenas with their backs that slope as if they're ashamed, slipping through the bush after the smell. If one turned its head, you saw it had big brown shining eyes like our own when we looked at each other in the dark. The wind brought voices in our own language from the compounds where the people who work in the camps live. A woman among us wanted to go to them at night and ask them to help us. They can give us the food from the dustbins, she said, she started wailing and our grandmother had to grab her and put a hand over her mouth. The man who led us had told us that we must keep out of the way of our people who worked at the Kruger Park; if they helped us they would lose their work. If they saw us, all they could do was pretend we were not there; they had seen only animals.

Sometimes we stopped to sleep for a little while at night. We slept close together. I don't know which night it was – because we were walking, walking, any time, all the time – we heard the lions very near. Not groaning loudly the way they did far off. Panting, like we do when we run, but it's a different kind of panting: you can hear they're not running, they're waiting, somewhere near. We all rolled closer together, on top of each other, the ones on the edge fighting to get into the middle. I was squashed against a woman who smelled bad because she was afraid but I was glad to hold tight on to her. I prayed to God to make the lions take someone on the edge and go. I shut my eyes not to see the tree from which a lion might jump right into the middle of us, where I was. The man who led us jumped up instead, and beat on the tree with a dead branch. He had taught us never to make a sound but he shouted. He shouted at the lions like a drunk man shouting at nobody, in our village. The lions went away. We heard them groaning, shouting back at him from far off.

We were tired, so tired. My first-born brother and the man had to lift our grandfather from stone to stone where we found places to cross the rivers. Our grandmother is strong but her feet were bleeding. We could not carry the basket on our heads any longer, we couldn't carry anything except my little brother. We left our things under a bush. As long as our bodies get there, our grandmother said. Then we ate some wild fruit we didn't know from home and our stomachs ran. We were in the grass called elephant grass because it is nearly as tall as an elephant, that day we had those pains, and our grandfather couldn't just get down in front of people like my little brother, he went off into the grass to be on his own. We had to keep up, the man who led us always kept telling us, we must catch up, but we asked him to wait for our grandfather.

So everyone waited for our grandfather to catch up. But he didn't. It was the middle of the day; insects were singing in our ears and we couldn't hear him moving through the grass. We couldn't see him because the grass was so high and he was so small. But he must have been somewhere there inside his loose trousers and his shirt that was torn and our grandmother couldn't sew because she had no cotton. We knew he couldn't have gone far because he was weak and slow. We all went to look for him, but in groups, so we too wouldn't be hidden from each other in that grass. It got into our eyes and noses; we called him softly but the noise of the insects must have filled the little space left for hearing in his ears. We looked and looked but we couldn't find him. We stayed in that long grass all night. In my sleep I found him curled round in a place he had tramped down for himself, like the places we'd seen where the buck hide their babies.

When I woke up he still wasn't anywhere. So we looked again, and by now there were paths we'd made by going through the grass many times, it would be easy for him to find us if we couldn't find him. All that day we just sat and waited. Everything is very quiet when the sun is on your head, inside your head, even if you lie, like the animals, under the trees. I lay on my back and saw those ugly birds with hooked beaks and plucked necks flying round and round above us. We had passed them often where they were feeding on the bones of dead animals, nothing was ever left there for us to eat. Round and round, high up and then lower down and then high again. I saw their necks poking to this side and that. Flying round and round. I saw our grandmother, who sat up all the time with my little brother on her lap, was seeing them, too.

In the afternoon the man who led us came to our grandmother and told her the other people must move on. He said, If their children don't eat soon they will die.

Our grandmother said nothing.

I'll bring you water before we go, he told her.

Our grandmother looked at us, me, my first-born brother, and my little brother on her lap. We watched the other people getting up to leave. I didn't believe the grass would be empty, all around us, where they had been. That we would be alone in this place, the Kruger Park, the police or the animals would find us. Tears came out of my eyes and nose onto my hands but our grandmother took no notice. She got up, with her feet apart the way she puts them when she is going to lift firewood, at home in our village, she swung my little brother onto her back, tied him in her cloth – the top of her dress was torn and her big breasts were showing but there was nothing in them for him. She said, Come.

So we left the place with the long grass. Left behind. We went with the others and the man who led us. We started to go away, again.

There's a very big tent, bigger than a church or a school, tied down to the ground. I didn't understand that was what it would be, when we got there, away. I saw a thing like that the time our mother took us to the town because she heard our soldiers were there and she wanted to ask them if they knew where our father was. In that tent, people were praying and singing. This one is blue and white like that one but it's not for praying and singing, we live in it with other people who've come from our country. Sister from the clinic says we're two hundred

A family at a refugee camp.

without counting the babies, and we have new babies, some were born on the way through the Kruger Park.

Inside, even when the sun is bright it's dark and there's a kind of whole village in there. Instead of houses each family has a little place closed off with sacks or cardboard from boxes – whatever we can find – to show the other families it's yours and they shouldn't come in even though there's no door and no windows and no thatch, so that if you're standing up and you're not a small child you can see into everybody's house. Some people have even made paint from ground rocks and drawn designs on the sacks.

Of course, there really is a roof – the tent is the roof, far, high up. It's like a sky. It's like a mountain and we're inside it; through the cracks paths of dust lead down, so thick you think you could climb them. The tent keeps off the rain overhead but the water comes in at the sides and in the little streets between our places – you can only move along them one person at a time – the small kids like my little brother play in the mud. You have to step over them. My little brother doesn't play. Our grandmother takes him to the clinic when the doctor comes on Mondays. Sister says there's something wrong with his head, she thinks it's because we didn't have enough food at home. Because of the war. Because our father wasn't there. And then because he was so hungry in the Kruger Park. He likes just to lie about on our grandmother all day, on her lap or against her somewhere, and he looks at us and looks at us. He wants to ask something but you can see he can't. If I tickle him he may just smile. The clinic gives us special powder to make into porridge for him and perhaps one day he'll be all right.

When we arrived we were like him – my first-born brother and I. I can hardly remember. The people who live in the village near the tent took us to the clinic, it's where you have to sign that you've come – away, through the Kruger Park. We sat on the grass and everything was muddied. One Sister was pretty with her hair straightened and beautiful high-heeled shoes and she brought us the special powder. She said we must mix it with water and drink it slowly. We tore the packets open with our teeth and licked it all up, it stuck round my mouth and I sucked it from my lips and fingers. Some other children who had walked with us vomited. But I only felt everything in my belly moving, the stuff going down and around like a snake, and hiccups hurt me. Another Sister called us to stand in line on the verandah of the clinic but we couldn't. We sat all over the place there, falling against each other; the Sisters helped each of us up by the arm and then stuck a needle in it. Other needles drew our blood into tiny bottles. This was against sickness, but I didn't understand, every time my eyes dropped closed I thought I was walking, the grass was long, I saw the elephants, I didn't know we were away.

But our grandmother was still strong, she could still stand up, she know how to write and she signed for us. Our grandmother got us this place in the tent against one of the sides, it's the best kind of place there because although the rain comes in, we can lift the flap when the weather is good and then the sun shines on us, the smells in the tent go out. Our grandmother knows a woman here who showed her where there is good grass for sleeping mats, and our grandmother made some for us. Once every month the food truck comes to the clinic. Our grandmother takes along one of the cards she signed and when it has been punched we get a sack of mealie meal. There are wheelbarrows to take it back to the tent; my first-born brother does this for her and then he and the other boys have races, steering the empty wheelbarrows back to the clinic. Sometimes he's lucky and a man who's bought beer in the village gives him money to deliver it – though that's not allowed, you're supposed to take that wheelbarrow straight back to the Sisters. He buys a cold drink and shares it with me if I catch him. On another day, every month, the church leaves a pile of old clothes in the clinic yard. Our grandmother has another card to get punched, and then we can choose something: I have two dresses, two pants and a jersey, so I can go to school.

The people in the village have let us join their school. I was surprised to find they speak our language; our grandmother told me, That's why they allow us to stay on their land. Long ago, in the time of our fathers, there was no fence that kills you, there was no Kruger Park between them and us, we were the same people under our own king, right from our village we left to this place we've come to.

Now that we've been in the tent so long – I have turned eleven and my little brother is nearly three although he is so small, only his head is big, he's not come right in it yet – some people have dug up the bare ground around the tent and planted beans and mealies and cabbage. The old men weave branches to put up fences round their gardens. No one is allowed to look for work in the towns but some of the women have found work in the village and can buy things. Our grandmother, because she's still strong, finds work where people are building houses – in this village the people build nice houses with bricks and cement, not mud like we used to have at our home. Our grandmother carries bricks for these people and fetches baskets of stones on her head. And so she has money to buy sugar and tea and milk and soap. The store gave her a calendar she has hung up on our flap of the tent. I am clever at school and she collected advertising paper people throw away outside the store and covered my schoolbooks with it. She makes my first-born brother and me do our homework every afternoon before it gets dark because there is no room except to lie down, close together, just as we did in the Kruger Park, in our place in the tent, and candles are expensive. Our grandmother hasn't been able to buy herself a pair of shoes for church yet, but she has bought black school shoes and polish to clean them with for my first-born brother and me. Every morning when people are getting up in the tent, the babies are crying, people are pushing each other at the taps outside and some children are already pulling the crusts of porridge off the pots we ate from last night, my first-born brother and I clean our shoes. Our grandmother makes us sit on our mats with our legs straight out so she can look carefully at our shoes to make sure we have done it properly. No other children in the tent have real school shoes. When we three look at them it's as if we are in a real house again, with no war, no away.

Some white people came to take photographs of our people living in the tent – they said they were making a film, I've never seen what that is though I know about it. A white woman squeezed into our space and asked our grandmother questions which were told to us in our language by someone who understands the white woman's.

How long have you been living like this?

She means here? our grandmother said. In this tent, two years and one month.

And what do you hope for the future?

Nothing. I'm here.

But for your children?

I want them to learn so that they can get good jobs and money.

Do you hope to go back to Mozambique – to your own country?

I will not go back.

But when the war is over – you won't be allowed to stay here? Don't you want to go home?

I didn't think our grandmother wanted to speak again. I didn't think she was going to answer the white woman. The white woman put her head on one side and smiled at us.

Our grandmother looked away from her and spoke – There is nothing. No home.

Why does our grandmother say that? Why? I'll go back. I'll go back through that Kruger Park. After the war, if there are no bandits any more, our mother may be waiting for us. And maybe when we left our grandfather, he was only left behind, he found his way somehow, slowly, through the Kruger Park, and he'll be there. They'll be home, and I'll remember them.

Further reading

The Ultimate Safari comes from a collection called *Jump and Other Stories* (Bloomsbury Publishing PLC, 2003). You might enjoy other stories in this collection, such as *The Moment Before the Gun Went Off* and the horrifying fairy tale *Once upon a Time*.

Me, a Mother at 15? No Way!

by Jeremy Hart

This article from the *Independent* newspaper describes a youth club's imaginative project aimed at bringing home some of the pressures and strains of becoming a parent.

Looking after a computerised 'living doll' is making teenage girls in Lincolnshire think twice about unprotected sex.

Not 60 minutes in her teenage mother's arms, 7 lb Dana Katherine has already been abused. She's not bruised, she doesn't even cry, but a red light in her computerised brain is flashing, evidence that she has had a rough start to life with Katie Hudson, her 15-year-old mother.

Petite and fragile, Katie doesn't look capable of hurting a baby, but she is furious. She is taking her first 48 hours of motherhood very seriously, so when a jealous nine-year-old cousin hits Dana's realistically scrunched-up vinyl face, baby and mother see red.

Dana, her name only for the two days she is in the normally tender care of auburn-haired Katie, is one of 100 computerised dolls recently imported from inventor Richard Jurmain, from San Diego, in an attempt to help cut Britain's teenage pregnancy rate, the highest in Europe.

Bought by schools, youth clubs and children's homes, the lifelike £150 babies are being used to give teenage volunteers the short, sharp shock of early parenthood, without any of the joy.

Looking, feeling and, at first, sounding like the real thing, Baby Think It Over is a nerve-jangling deterrent. 'Two days with that was enough to make anyone think hard about unprotected sex,' says Dawne Spiller, Dana's first mother in Boston, Lincolnshire.

A stressful six times a day, for up to 35 minutes a time, Dana is programmed to emit an ear-piercing cry. She will only stop when her mother inserts a plastic key into her back, simulating the relief of a bottle or a change of nappy.

'No one likes to be woken at five o'clock in the morning, especially teenagers, and not by a crying baby,' says Anne Dorrian, the Lincolnshire County Council Youth Officer who saw the computer infants on the *Oprah Winfrey Show* and decided to order one for her Focus One youth club in Boston.

Focus One is a sparkling oasis in the drab crime-ridden surroundings of the Fenland town's Woad Farm Estate, a magnet for bored teenagers whose alternative attraction is petty crime. Former members include the Aston Villa footballer Julian Joachim, and the club is more of a home to the 60 members than some of their dysfunctional homes.

Lincolnshire is in the top ten per cent for teenage births in Britain, itself with the worst record in Europe. Almost nine in every 1,000 teenage girls in the UK become pregnant between the ages of 13 and 15.

Ignorance and peer pressure are the prime causes of underage pregnancies . . . Many girls known to Focus One members are reportedly raped without recognising it as rape.

'There is one girl at school who was pregnant at 13,' says Katie, as she wheels Dana through the crowds in Boston's Saturday market in search of baby food and clothes while her friends gather, tribally, outside McDonald's and the music shop.

'She came to school until she had the baby and then came back once she had had it. The father is 15. I feel sorry for her. When she came up town, all these people would look at her. She had a life ahead of her. Now that's gone.'

Katie is the first volunteer in the club who doesn't have a boyfriend. 'I'm just in between relationships,' she jokes, but only half-heartedly. Katie would rather have a boyfriend and suffer all the inherent sexual tensions that come with a teenage romance than traipse the streets of thirties semis at night with her girlfriends.

The clock in the town centre chimes 10 am. It is almost 15 hours since Anne Dorrian handed Katie her baby for a weekend of disturbed and deprived sleep. Dana has been silent for two hours while Katie and her firends Lisa and Tracey have trundled through Boston's shops. Then, as if Dana is waiting for the most embarrassing place to let rip, she lets out her metallic cry like an irritating public-address announcement in the coffee shop of the town's department store.

Lisa and Tracey bolt for the ladies while Katie frantically rips off Dana's sleepsuit and inserts the key. 'Bloody chickens,' she mutters, as her friends cower in the cubicles. As Dana cries, on and off for more than half an hour, two old ladies peer over Katie's shoulder and coo. 'Ah,' one says. Katie bursts out laughing. It is bad enough that the doll makes a noise, let alone that anyone thinks it real.

'Last night we just hung around the estate and Dana didn't cry at all. I thought she might be broken or something,' says Katie, black shadows under her eyes. 'Then as Tracey and I were walking home from Lisa's, she started crying.

'We panicked. If you don't get her clothes off and put the key in within a minute, the computer says that you have abused the baby. It started crying at 10.55 and stopped about twenty past eleven.'

Katie had resisted her maternal urge to rock the doll as its recorded screech echoed around her parent's simply decorated semi-detached council house. 'Only the key stops the crying, but Mum said I should rock it anyway. I had cramp in my fingers when she finally stopped.' Katie had to hold the key in Dana's back rather than leave the key in her and lie her on her front. If the baby is lain on her front she will cry until the batteries run out.

Never normally in bed before the small hours, Katie and Tracey (who had volunteered to sleep over and help Katie through the ordeal) were still awake when Dana's body clock rang again.

'We were watching *Hotel Babylon* with Dani Behr when she went off again. That time it only lasted 15 minutes. The longer between cries, the longer each cry lasts.'

Asleep in the living room, so as not to wake her parents, Katie and Tracey had a full four hours' sleep before Dana's dawn chorus. 'I didn't even hear her cry,' admits Katie, suddenly adopting a more personal view to her not-so-cuddly charge. 'Tracey had to wake me up. Because the key was fixed to my wrist, I was the only one who would stop Dana crying.'

Katie's selfless attitude towards the rest of the house's slumber seemed to work. Her mother, Debbie, likes the doll. 'It takes me back a while,' she says.

At Dawne Spiller's house a few weeks ago, Dana was not a welcome addition. 'On the Saturday night Mum said I had to sleep round the neighbours' house 'cause she couldn't stand the noise,' shrugs Dawne, 14. 'She said it's either there or out in the garden shed.'

Being woken three times each night also got on Dawne's nerves. 'She really riled me after a while. I was out uptown with my mates when it started crying. I hit it because I was embarrassed. I swore at her and told her to shut up. I almost threw it in the bin. When Sunday night came I was so happy to give it back.'

Anne Dorrian was just as relieved to see Dawne's reaction as Dawne was to get rid of the doll. She had taken a gamble when she bought it and had no plans to force the girls to take it home. 'I had worried that the baby wouldn't work, wouldn't provoke such a response from the girls, but it did and has done with the other four who have had it.' Dorrian has recommended the doll for Lincolnshire's other 23 youth clubs.

Although many of the teenagers at Focus One are in sexual relationships, Dana is not directly responsible for preventing any pregnancies as yet, and definitely no thanks to the girls' boyfriends.

'The boys thought it was a big joke and hit the doll,' says Sinead, whose boyfriend, Jonathan, is 18. 'They don't have to bear the consequences of getting pregnant. You have to be careful anyway and, after living with the baby for two days it really makes you be more careful. I would like to have kids, but not at 15.'

Focus One, like the majority of organisations using Baby Think It Over, has no plans to let the baby loose on boys. 'They have too much testosterone coursing through their veins and are too image-conscious to walk around Boots with a baby for the weekend. It will take a lot of education to get them ready for this,' says Dorrian, herself a single mother of two.

Having a baby cousin, Katie is used to the tiring and meticulous routine of parenthood. 'I've helped look after my cousins with nappy changing and bathing,' she says. It's ironic then that during her two days of computer parenting she did not wipe Dana's face once or find her a change of clothes.

'I didn't have time this morning and yesterday I forgot,' she admits after her first night of interrupted sleep. 'I was too focused on its crying to worry about anything else.'

In fact, the dolls are free of many of the irksome ingredients of early life such as sterilising, nappy-changing, washing, projectile vomiting, colic and nappy rash.

'The idea is to give them a shock of the routine needed to look after a baby,' says Dorrian. 'Of course, we could make them sterilise bottles or change nappies, but make the test too hard and you won't get any volunteers.'

Up town in Boots, Katie and Tracey are checking the prices of baby food and clothes against the estimates they had made a few days earlier. For 432 jars of baby food, Katie had reckoned on £30. 'I was a little bit out,' she winces, obviously more used to pricing CDs and jeans. The actual cost: £159.84. 'Babies cost a lot don't they?'

and what's more ...
Britain has the worst teenage pregnancy record in Europe. Almost nine in every 1,000 teenage girls in the UK become pregnant between the ages of 13 and 15. The latest statistics were compiled in 1993 when the highest rates of teenage pregnancy were found in Barnsley (16.5 per 1,000). The lowest rates were found in the South-west (3.4 per 1,000).

Further reading

In Anne Fine's novel *Flour Babies* (Longman, 1996) a class of teenagers – boys and girls – are given bags of flour which they have to look after for several weeks, making sure they don't get damaged, and never leaving them on their own. They soon learn what commitment to a baby really means . . .

The Sorrows of Sandra Saint
by Lee Hall

> Lee Hall's play was first performed on Radio 4 in 1997 as part of a series called *God's Country*, which focused on children dealing with crises in their lives.
>
> Fourteen-year-old Sandra and her twelve-year-old brother Scout are struggling to recover from their father's death. Sandra has just discovered that she's pregnant . . .

Characters

SANDRA A girl
SCOUT (STEPHEN)   Her brother
MAM   Her mum

Scout's bedroom

SCOUT   Dad, if you can hear this. First, I hope you're alright and that. We miss you, you know that. And second, I just wanted to ask you, if there's any way of making Sandra be nice to uz, that would be very good indeed. She's always been quite horrible. But after what happened, she's been getting at uz like something rotten. That's all really. But, and I know this sounds daft and everything, if there's any way of coming back to see uz . . . even for a bit . . . well . . . anyway, I have to go.

MUSIC: *'To Know Him Is to Love Him'* – The Teddy Bears.

Sandra's bedroom

The music fades, but plays under Sandra's next speech.

SANDRA   *(Reading)* What you may be feeling. Emotionally: instability comparable to pre-menstrual tension, irritability, mood swings, weepiness, misgivings, fear, joy, periodic elation, depression. Physically: fatigue, tiredness, frequent urination, occasional vomiting, heartburn, indigestion, food aversions, breast changes, amenorrhoea – absence of menstruation. *(Expostulating)* Jesus Christ!

A few bars of music.

Scout's bedroom

SCOUT   Do you miss him?
SANDRA   Dad?
        Pause.
SCOUT   I mean do you talk to him?
SANDRA   Don't be stupid.
SCOUT   It's not stupid. It's what the counsellor said.
SANDRA   The counsellor?
SCOUT   It's supposed to help things.
SANDRA   What's that going to help?
SCOUT   Coming to terms with it or something.
SANDRA   It doesn't help anything.
SCOUT   I talk to him.
SANDRA   Jesus Christ.
SCOUT   I knew you'd laugh.
SANDRA   I wasn't laughing ... What do you say?
SCOUT   I don't know. All sorts. What I've had for dinner, what's on telly. Normal stuff.
SANDRA   What's on telly?
SCOUT   Well.
SANDRA   He doesn't want to know what's on telly, man. He's dead.
        Long pause.
SCOUT   I was only doing what they said.
SANDRA   That's your trouble isn't it?
SCOUT   What's wrong with that?
SANDRA   You end up talking to dead people for a start.
SCOUT   Well, I miss him.
SANDRA   So do I, but it doesn't mean I have to delude myself.

SCOUT   But haven't I got a right to delude myself? I'm only twelve.
SANDRA   Well, I'm only fourteen.
SCOUT   Well. There's a big difference.
SANDRA   The difference is you won't face up to things.
SCOUT   Mam does it.
SANDRA   Exactly.
SCOUT   At least I try.
SANDRA   What's that meant to mean?
SCOUT   Mam says you need to get a hobby or something.
SANDRA   Just because you're in the Scouts doesn't make you better than me.
SCOUT   I never said it did.
SANDRA   You think you're king dick with all them badges.
SCOUT   It's not my fault I go to Scouts.
SANDRA   Who's fault is it then?
SCOUT   You could go to Guides.
SANDRA   I don't want to go to Guides.
SCOUT   Well, why are you complaining then?
SANDRA   Just admit it. She hates me.
SCOUT   She doesn't hate you. She doesn't hate anyone.
SANDRA   I'm not stupid.
SCOUT   Please Sandra.
SANDRA   You hate uz.
SCOUT   How?
SANDRA   The way you sit there and let me get picked on.
SCOUT   But I don't pick on you.
SANDRA   You just sit there like a little smug bastard.
SCOUT   It's just the way I look . . .
SANDRA   I don't see why I have to get the blame.
SCOUT   But nobody's giving you the blame.
SANDRA   I was the one who had to help him.
SCOUT   Don't.
SANDRA   With all the blood and everything. And you and her sit there like butter wouldn't melt in your mouth.
SCOUT   If you hadn't have run out, he would have never got hit.

SANDRA   So it *was* my fault?
         Pause.
SCOUT   No. It was nobody's fault.
SANDRA   Is that what Mam told you to say?
SCOUT   It's the truth.
SANDRA   It's not what she thinks though.
SCOUT   Well, what do you expect?
SANDRA   There. You see. It wasn't my fault I ran out. Things just happen. What if he had woke up the next day and got cancer, or fell down the stairs? Anything can happen . . .
         Pause.
SCOUT   What do you think happens when you die?
SANDRA   Nothing.
SCOUT   So you think I should give up talking to him?
SANDRA   Well, you can't bring him back to life.
SCOUT   Why are you so angry at everything?
SANDRA   I'm not angry.
SCOUT   Oh.
SANDRA   I just hate things that don't make sense.
SCOUT   Like Dad?
SANDRA   Dad makes perfect sense. He had an accident and died. I mean people.
SCOUT   I don't know what you mean.
SANDRA   That's your problem.
         MUSIC: 'Come See about Me' – Diana Ross and the Supremes.

Sandra's bedroom

SANDRA   *(Reading)* Things you should do. In the first few months you will need a lot of emotional support. Feel free to share your feelings with people around you. If you feel worried or nervous be sure to talk to someone close to you. Avoid stress. Your body is out of balance. Try not to enter into situations or conversations that you normally find difficult. Take constant rests if you feel tired.

If a nap at the office is not a reasonable goal, be sure there is a place you can sit and unwined undisturbed. Let others baby you – perhaps your mother-in-law will do the ironing, perhaps your husband will take on some of the domestic duties.

The kitchen

MAM   Would you like a biscuit? I just bought a packet.
SCOUT   What of?
MAM   Fig rolls.
SCOUT   But I hate fig rolls.
MAM   Where have they gone?
SCOUT   Why did you buy fig rolls?
MAM   I thought you liked them.
SCOUT   I hate them.
MAM   Well, that's news to me. You used to eat them.
SCOUT   Fig rolls?
MAM   Yes, fig rolls.
SCOUT   When?
MAM   All the time.
SCOUT   Sausage rolls.
MAM   What are you on about sausage rolls? I used to give you fig rolls when you went to camp.
SCOUT   Custard creams.
MAM   Custard creams?
SCOUT   You should get custard creams.
MAM   Where are they?
SCOUT   Where are what?
MAM   The fig rolls. They've disappeared.
SCOUT   But I don't want a fig roll.
MAM   Have you been eating them?
SCOUT   Mam.
MAM   It's Sandra, isn't it? I've told her.
SCOUT   Has she eaten them?
MAM   There was a whole packet here yesterday. Look.
The sound of a tin being opened.

MAM	There's nothing there. She'll blow up like a balloon. Where is she?
SCOUT	I don't know.
MAM	She's driving me round the twist.
SCOUT	I think she's at Karen's.
MAM	Maybe there's something I've done? Tell me. Is there something I've done?
SCOUT	I don't know.
MAM	What more can I do, Stephen?
SCOUT	Maybe she was hungry.
MAM	It's attention seeking. There was a whole packet in there.
SCOUT	Maybe she's bulimic.
MAM	She's not bulimic, she's a bloody menace.
SCOUT	It's only a packet of biscuits.
MAM	It's not the biscuits. It's her attitude. Take, take, take. Stephen, I'm doing everything I can. I'm at my rope's end.
SCOUT	Look, Mam, forget about the biscuits. I'll go to the shop. *(The sound of the door opening. Sandra comes in.)*
MAM	Here she is – Miss Biscuit.
SCOUT	Mam.
MAM	Where have you been?
SANDRA	Out.
MAM	Where?
SANDRA	Just about.
MAM	Have you been with that Karen Atkinson?
SANDRA	We were doing our homework.
MAM	Till ten o'clock at night? *(Pause)* And what do you make of this?
	The sound of a tin being opened.
SANDRA	Make of what?
MAM	This.
SANDRA	It's empty.
MAM	Exactly.
SANDRA	So?

MAM	Well, where did they go?
SANDRA	What go?
MAM	The fig rolls.
SANDRA	Fig rolls?
MAM	Don't play the innocent with me. I put them there yesterday.
SANDRA	Fig rolls?
MAM	You ate the bloody lot of them . . .
SANDRA	Do you really think I'm going to eat a whole packet of fig rolls?
MAM	Well, what have you done with them?
SANDRA	I haven't done anything.
SCOUT	But . . .
SANDRA	*(To Scout)* Shut up, you.
MAM	I'm sure I bought them.
SANDRA	You know what, Mam? You're doolally. You never bought any biscuits yesterday. You don't know what you're doing and then go round blaming people willy-nilly.
MAM	I do not blame people willy-nilly.
SANDRA	Well, why are you on my back?
MAM	Because you go round acting like a selfish little cow.
SANDRA	So that means I stole your biscuits?
MAM	I don't know what it means, Sandra, but it's got to stop.
SANDRA	Well, it won't stop until you start being reasonable. You probably ate them yourself judging by the size of you.
MAM	Oh, get out.
SANDRA	That's where I was going in the first place. *(To Scout)* And wipe that smile off your face.
SCOUT	I haven't got a smile on my face.
SANDRA	It's a good job as well. *Sound of Sandra going out.*
MAM	I don't know what's got into her.
SCOUT	Mam, did you buy those biscuits? *Long pause.*

MAM (*Unsure*) Course I did.
     MUSIC: *Introduction to 'Back in My Arms Again' – Diana Ross and The Supremes.*

Sandra's bedroom

SANDRA (*Reading*) What to eat. The principles of nine months' healthy eating. (*She reads with gradually increasing horror.*) Every bite counts. Every meal you eat contributes to giving your child the best possible start in life. Remember now you are eating for two. To give your baby that kick start into health and happiness you must start eating a balanced diet.

Protein: four servings a day. Foods high in protein include nuts and seeds, whole grain baked goods, soy beans, yoghurt, hard-boiled eggs and wheatgerm. Vitamin C rich foods. Have at least two of the following: half a grapefruit, two small oranges, a half pound of shredded cabbage or a bowl of raw spinach. Whole grains and legumes, six to eleven servings per day: mung beans, millet, bulgar wheat, buckwheat groats, peas, butter beans or couscous. Bloody Hell!

MUSIC: *'Back in My Arms Again' – Diana Ross and the Supremes.*

The living room

MAM (*On the phone*) I am trying, Mam. It's . . . you don't understand what she's like . . . No, I am not making a mountain out of a mole hill . . . You don't understand. I don't know what to do with her . . . All right, I will. I'll talk to her . . . (*Getting irritated*) All right, I said I would talk to her . . . Yes, OK. (*Sound of the door opening. Scout comes in.*) Jesus Christ! (*On the phone*) I have to go. (*To Scout*) What the hell's happened to you?

SCOUT I fell in the river, Mam.

MAM You're soaked. Are you all right?
SCOUT I was pulled out by this lad. He said he was an angel.
MAM You better get these clothes off. You're covered in gunk.
SCOUT I know.
MAM You didn't swallow anything did you?
SCOUT I had my mouth shut.
MAM What were you doing down by the river anyway?
SCOUT Practising knots.
MAM Well, I think you should stay home in future, sweetheart. *(She gets a towel.)* Here, let's dry you off.
SCOUT Mam, do you still talk to Dad?
MAM Sometimes.
Pause.
SCOUT He doesn't answer you though, does he?
MAM Not in the normal sense.
SCOUT Mam, do you think he can really hear?
MAM I don't know, love. But there's no harm in trying.
SCOUT I suppose so . . . Mam, do you blame Sandra for what happened?
MAM Of course I don't.
SCOUT Do you hate her?
Pause.
MAM Of course, I don't hate her . . . it's just –
SCOUT What?
MAM I think you should go and get dry.
MUSIC: *'To Know Him Is to Love Him'* – The Teddy Bears.

Sandra's bedroom

A knock on the door.
MAM Sandra, I've been thinking and I think we should talk.
SANDRA What about?
MAM About this problem.
SANDRA What problem?
MAM It doesn't have to be like this. I know I've been on edge – after what happened. And I realise that it hasn't been very easy for any of us.

SANDRA	It's been quite simple for me.
MAM	Sandra, it can't be simple. Death isn't simple. You can't just shut off from it.
SANDRA	That's what I'm trying to tell you. I'm not shut off from it, I've just come to terms with it.
MAM	But you go around as if you couldn't care less. It's not good for you.
SANDRA	Don't tell me, what's good for uz. I'm the only one who's got over it.
MAM	You haven't got over it.
SANDRA	Yes, I have. Because I don't feel guilty.
MAM	What's that meant to mean?
SANDRA	Just what I said.
MAM	Guilty about what?
SANDRA	For God's sake mother.
MAM	I come up here to make things easier for us and suddenly you go and start saying things like that.
SANDRA	Well, it's true.
MAM	Nothing's true. What do you mean, guilty?
SANDRA	It's true.
MAM	Well, everybody feels guilty. Some guilt.
SANDRA	Not necessarily.
MAM	Well, they should. Everybody's a bit guilty.
SANDRA	Here we go.
MAM	What do you mean?
SANDRA	You just want someone else to blame. Someone to alleviate your shoulders.
MAM	You don't sound clever, you know.
SANDRA	You think it was me, don't you? *Slight pause.*
MAM	I don't think it was anybody. *(Pause)* Sandra, I love you. You know that.
SANDRA	Do you? *Pause.*
MAM	Of course I do. And the only way through this is to pull together and –

SANDRA   And what?
MAM   Speak frankly.
SANDRA   I am speaking frankly.
MAM   You're not, Sandra, all you're doing is going round in circles. You're picking at me. It's like this all day long. We all know how clever you are. You don't have to prove it by shooting everyone else down.
SANDRA   Sorry.
MAM   Listen to you, you're not sorry.
SANDRA   But you slept with that man, didn't you?
MAM   What man?
SANDRA   In the office.
MAM   That has nothing to do with it.
SANDRA   But it's true though.
MAM   It was years ago. It had nothing to do with you or Dad or Stephen or any of you. It was a mistake.
SANDRA   You bet.
MAM   This is impossible.
SANDRA   You know . . . the thing is . . . what you're trying to do . . . because everything in your life is out of control . . . everything is in chaos . . . you're trying to control us. You're trying to make us the perfect little things you'd like the world to be. And good little Stephen does his best, but I'm not living my life out for you.
MAM   I can't just let this go, the way you're behaving. *(Pause)* I think you're still grieving.
SANDRA   So are you.
MAM   Of course I am.
SANDRA   Do you think this started just because he died? Mam, I'm not a kid any more.
MAM   Oh, Sandra.
SANDRA   Oh, Sandra what?
MAM   Why are you doing this?
SANDRA   Doing what?
MAM   Pushing me.

SANDRA	I'm not pushing anybody. You're pushing yourself.
MAM	I'm just trying to be reasonable.
SANDRA	It's a bit late for that.
MAM	Do you know, anyone else would have thumped you by now.
SANDRA	What's stopping you?
MAM	Oh, stop it.
SANDRA	Stop what?
MAM	Oh, don't be ridiculous, Sandra.
SANDRA	Go on, hit me. See what that would prove.
MAM	Oh shut up.
SANDRA	Go on.
MAM	*(Screaming)* Oh stop it! Stop it! *(Calmer)* I don't want to have to shout at you. I don't want to have you hate me. I didn't want him to die. I don't want you to feel guilty. I don't want to force you into something. I don't want you to feel alone. Sandra, I've known you since you were a tiny child, and this is not you. For God's sake, I know I've screwed up enough over the last six months but surely you're intelligent enough to see I'm falling apart. You might think this is weird but I need you, Sandra. I need you. I can't lose you as well. *Pause.*
SANDRA	Mam, I'm pregnant. *Pause.*
MAM	Don't be stupid. *Slight pause.*
SANDRA	I'm not being stupid.
MAM	But what do you mean?
SANDRA	I took a test. I'm late.
MAM	But . . .
SANDRA	By two months. *Long pause.*
MAM	Oh my God – Why didn't you say any of this before?

SANDRA Say what?
MAM   Have you seen a doctor?
SANDRA How could I say something? I knew you'd go ballistic.
MAM   I'm not going ballistic. Am I?
SANDRA Look, you're starting.
MAM   I'm not starting anything.
SANDRA You never understand, do you?
MAM   I'm trying to understand. Sandra – you're fourteen.
SANDRA So?
MAM   Why didn't you use protection?
SANDRA It just happened.
MAM   Jesus Christ, Sandra. It doesn't just happen.
SANDRA Of course, it doesn't just happen. But it did happen.
MAM   Who's responsible?
SANDRA I am.
MAM   But who was the boy?
SANDRA What's that got to do with it?
MAM   Sandra.
SANDRA It could have been anybody.
MAM   Oh God, Sandra.
SANDRA You see? No wonder I haven't told you.
MAM   You have to tell me who it is.
SANDRA I don't know. I don't care. Do you think I want any of those poxy twerps having anything to do with it?
MAM   Twerps?
SANDRA I'm not having them bringing it up.
MAM   Bringing what up?
SANDRA The baby.
MAM   What baby?
SANDRA What baby do you think?
MAM   Sandra, there isn't going to be any baby.
SANDRA Mam, hasn't anybody explained the basic facts of human reproduction to you?
MAM   It's illegal. I mean –
SANDRA What?
MAM   You'll have to get rid of it.

SANDRA	I'm not getting rid of anything. It's my life. It's my baby.
MAM	Sandra. This is a perfectly respectable household. Things like this don't happen.
SANDRA	Oh?
MAM	You're acting like some slut from Walker.
SANDRA	Why can they have babies and I shouldn't?
MAM	They shouldn't be having babies either. Nobody should be having babies – nobody's gonna have babies. You're getting rid of it.
SANDRA	See, you're going ballistic.
MAM	*(Ballistic)* I am not going ballistic.
SANDRA	This is my choice – you've got nothing to do with it.
MAM	But you can have a child any time. You don't have to choose to have it now. You're too young, Sandra. *(Pause)* You'll ruin your life.
SANDRA	Did I ruin your life, then?
	Pause.
MAM	Sandra, I was twenty-three.
SANDRA	What's that got to do with it?
MAM	You're not finished school. You haven't even done your mocks yet.
SANDRA	I don't care about my mocks.
MAM	If you think having a baby's a way of getting out of your revision, you've got another think coming.
SANDRA	I'll do them later.
MAM	You need to think this through.
SANDRA	I have thought it through. When it goes to nursery, I'll do them at the college.
MAM	You haven't thought anything through. It's obvious.
SANDRA	Because if I'd thought anything through, I'd get rid of it – what sort of argument's that?
MAM	A damn good one.
SANDRA	It's not an argument. It's a plain assertion.
MAM	You're just a child.
SANDRA	If I'm just a child, how the hell am I pregnant?

MAM   Oh, you're being ridiculous.
SANDRA   That is not ridiculous. You just don't want to admit it.
MAM   Let's look at this objectively.
SANDRA   OK.
MAM   Well . . .
SANDRA   Well what?
MAM   If you have this child now you'll mess up the next few years at school.
SANDRA   That's subjective.
MAM   It's not subjective.
SANDRA   Yes it is.
MAM   You can't go to school.
SANDRA   What about women with jobs?
MAM   Sandra.
SANDRA   What about single mothers?
MAM   So you'd rather be a single mother on the dole for the rest of your life?
SANDRA   Who's talking about the rest of my life? By the time I'm your age my child will have finished university.
MAM   You can't do this to me.
SANDRA   I'm not doing anything to you. You're doing it to yourself.
MAM   I'm the only one who's going to be left looking after it.
SANDRA   You don't have to do anything, if that's the way you feel.
MAM   That's not the way I feel.
SANDRA   What do you feel?
MAM   Oh Jesus, I don't know.
SANDRA   You know how stupid I am? There was part of uz that actually thought you might be pleased.
MAM   How could you think I could be happy?
SANDRA   That there was life after Dad.
MAM   What's that got to do with it?
SANDRA   That there's some hope, you know. That things don't have to stop. Like there's some bigger purpose than having to get on with domestic science or

worrying about biscuits. I just thought there might be something. I thought you might realise you can't just plan things out neat, 'cos the world isn't like that, because there's more to life than just choosing a university, you know. Because you could wake up one morning and be run over by a bus. And if all you're worried about is how to pay the mortgage or that you wished you were better insured, well then you're already dead, Mam. Because life's about what you feel inside, life's about passions and caring for people, life's about creating things and moving on, not stopping them dead. Life's about saying screw you to the things that are trying to wring it out of you, life's about babies and having sex and hormones, a long time before GCSEs were invented or mortgages or Child Benefit. Life's wonderful and difficult and complicated.

MAM You don't have any idea what life's about . . .

Further reading

Spoonface Steinberg, Lee Hall's best-known radio monologue which is also part of the *God's Country* series, tells the poignant, painfully funny story of a young girl dying of cancer. You can read the script in *Spoonface Steinberg and Other Plays* (BBC Books, 1997) or listen to a recording (BBC Audiobooks Ltd, 1997).

Compass and Torch
by Elizabeth Baines

> Many of Elizabeth Baines' short stories are published on the web. They often look at the world through a child's eyes, and bring ordinary moments alive through their sharp detail. This one describes the painful tension between a boy and his estranged father on holiday together.

The road ends at a gate. The boy waits in the car while the man gets out. Beyond the gate is the open moor, pale in the early evening with bleached end-of-summer grass, bruised here and there with heather and age-old spills of purple granite. The boy, though, is not looking that way, ahead. He is watching the man: the way he strides to the gate, bouncing slightly in his boots, his calf-muscles flexing beneath the wide knee-length shorts, the flop of hair at the front and the close-shaved neck as he bends for the catch.

The boy is intent. Watching Dad. Watching what Dad is. Drinking it in: the essence of Dadness.

The man pushes the gate with one arm, abruptly, too hard – the boy misses a breath – and sure enough, the gate swings violently, bounces off the stone wall and begins to swing back again while the man is already returning to the car. But then it slows, keels out once more, and comes to rest, wide open, against the wall: the man judged correctly after all. The boy is relieved. And, as the man drops into the driving seat something in the boy's chest gives a little hop of joy and he cries excitedly, 'Oh, I brought my torch!'

Coming downstairs after finding his torch, he overheard his mother say what she thought of the expedition.

Mad, she was calling it, as he knew she would. 'Mad! The first time in four months he has his eight-year-old son and what does he plan to do? Take him camping up a mountain!

Talk about macho avoidance activity!' Her voice was low, and light and mocking, but he heard it catch, and he could also hear Jim, his mother's boyfriend who lived with them now, shifting at the kitchen table with an unhappy kind of rustle. His mother said: 'Well, what do you *expect?*' There was a choke in her voice now, and suddenly a kind of snarl: 'You wouldn't expect him to start *now*, would you – accommodating his child into his *life?*'

When the boy stepped into the kitchen he saw her start with alarm and shame. He said, 'I found my torch.'

'Oh good!' she said quickly, wrenching a look of bright enthusiasm onto her face.

The light seeping through her fuzzy hair made the bones of his shoulders ache.

Jim asked kindly, 'Is it all in working order?'

The boy forced himself to put the torch into Jim's big outstretched hand, to stand still and attentive while Jim gently twisted the barrel to make the bulb come on.

'It's a good one,' said Jim, pointedly approving, handing it back.

'Yes,' said the boy, forcing himself to acknowledge Jim's kindness and affirmation.

But Jim is not his dad.

'It's a red one,' he tells his dad now. 'It's in my rucksack.'

'Oh,' says his dad, 'good, good,' a little distractedly, driving the car quickly, efficiently through the gate. His dad parks the car neatly, gets out smartly and shuts the gate.

Some yards off on the tufted moor a scattered group of wild ponies lift their heads and sniff the air. One, dappled grey, moves with interest towards the car, man and boy.

The boy is still in the car, tugging at his rucksack, fighting with stiff straps to get at the torch. As the man comes back and puts his head into the open door, he holds it up: 'Here it is!'

'Great!' cries the man. He isn't looking at the torch.

He is looking away, seared by the glitter of anxiety in his little boy's eyes.

The horse comes up to the car. She nudges up, puts her nose over the edge of the door. The man bats her away.

It's OK, the boy decides, that his dad hasn't looked at the torch, hasn't studied or handled it like Jim. It's better: the torch is not for looking at now. It's better to have for it a proper purpose, to put it away, to carry it carelessly but with meaning, as a warrior might carry his sword. A torch is for lighting when the time comes, for lighting up the expedition of father and son.

'Come on!' says the man, all briskness now, and holds the door back for the boy to get out of the car.

Neither man nor boy take much notice of the horse. The man steps back, and she swings her head out of the way. They go to the boot, and after a moment she slowly follows.

The boy is chattering:

'Have you brought one too, have you brought a torch?'

'Oh, yes!'

Is this a problem? the boy suddenly wonders. Does this make one of the torches redundant? There is a brief moment of uncertainty.

'We can use both of them, can't we, Dad?'

'Oh, yes! Yes, of course!'

Then a swoop of delight: 'We can light up more with both, can't we?'

'Oh yes, certainly!' The man too is gratefully caught on a wave of triumph. 'Oh, yes, two are definitely better! Back-up, for a start.'

Two torches are for lighting a bigger space in the wilderness, for lighting it together. Two torches are for father and son to back each other up.

The man has swung up the car-boot door. The horse, softly curious, is standing behind.

'What colour is your torch, Dad?'

'Er . . .' The man is peering into the boot. 'Er . . . it's green.'

Unseen by the man and boy, clouds sweep like opening curtains above the brow of the hill and the grass lights up, bright yellow. Ancient rocks glint like heaving carcasses asleep.

Man and boy both peer intently into the boot. Behind them, the horse looks in too, through dark, deep-fringed eyes.

The man lifts up the tent in its smart holdall-style bag.

The boy still chatters. 'Is that the tent? What colour is it? Is it that round kind? Does it have a little porch?'

The man says with robust authority: 'It's an all-weather mountain tent. Two-man.'

The boy is thrilled. A tent to weather all conditions. In which he and his father will be two men.

The man looks up – for the first time – at the path they will take, which runs from the gate to the brow of the hill. Then he groans: 'I didn't bring a compass.'

The boy's eyes are suddenly wide with fear and dismay: not with the notion that they'll get lost, but because of the way the man's shoulders slumped and the tent in his hand dropped back onto the boot floor.

But then the man says quickly, almost brightly, 'Never mind!' and swings the tent out.

The boy breathes with relief. 'I've got a compass,' he cries, 'and guess what, I forgot mine too!'

He ought to have remembered it when he went upstairs for the torch. He might have thought of it if he hadn't already heard from his room the intent murmurings in the kitchen, and known the sort of thing his mother would be saying, and wanted badly to get back down there and make her stop.

No hope of him relating to his son on any personal, day-to-day level! No hope of him trying to RELATE to him!

The boy might have remembered it, the compass, as they were leaving. But he couldn't wait to get going, for it all to be over: the way his dad said, 'Hi there!' in that brittle, jovial way to Jim, and the way Jim dropped his eyes when he'd said Hi back, as if he understood all there was to understand about Dad, and didn't want to embarrass him by letting him know that. As if as well as despising him, Jim also – horribly – felt sorry for Dad. And the way his mother said hardly anything, and made her face blank whenever Dad spoke to her or looked her way, and kept shredding a tissue so bits leaked though her fingers to the floor. When they were ready for off she put her head in through the car window, and her eyes were bulging and wobbly with tears, and he thought he couldn't bear this: that this moment which he had looked forward to, longed for, as his moment of joy, was a moment of sadness for her. And that terrible thing she had said to Dad: 'Now you *will* be careful? Don't go camping too near the edge.' Unforgivable – as if she and Jim didn't think that Dad could think of such a thing for himself.

And then the worst thing of all: that brief but really awful moment when the car slid out of the drive and he felt, after all, he didn't want to go. That was another reason the compass never entered his head.

But they don't need a compass after all. They are adventurers, after all. Compasses are things that boys and dads tend to have, but which, when they are alert and strong at heart, they can leave behind. It is no accident that they both left their compasses behind.

'I keep mine by my bed,' he tells his dad. 'Where do you keep yours?'

'In my desk,' says the man.

The boy nods with satisfaction. He struggles unsuccessfully to get his arm in his rucksack strap; his arm flails.

The man's chest twists. He holds the strap wide so the boy can get his arm in. The horse nuzzles the rucksack top and the man pushes her away.

The horse sighs. She wheels around. Facing the open moor, she lifts her tail, spreads her hind legs and provides a close-up display which could easily fascinate an eight-year-old boy: opens and flexes her bright-red arse and lets out a steaming stream.

'Is it the kind of compass where the top lifts up, like mine?' asks the boy eagerly, with eyes only for the man.

As the stream goes on hitting the ground, the man snaps the boot shut, with satisfying clicks attaches sleeping bags and tent to his own pack, and shoulders the lot. The boy is gratified by his speed but unsettled by his subtle nervy hurry. The man checks the car locks. 'Right?' he says, and decisive, without looking round to check the boy is following, sets off.

Which is good, thinks the boy: no nonsense. There's an important adventure ahead, which means there's no time for hanging around. 'Right!' he echoes, and sets off too, running to catch up.

Neither looks back at the nestled shiny car, the snaking wall, the ghost-coloured ponies in the hummocky grass.

The man strides; the boy walks fast, gladly half-runs, proud to keep up. They reach the top in no time. When they get there, they do not stop, as most walkers there do, to take in the view, the purple sweep of the plain towards the blue wall of mountains beyond. They keep going, and the boy is asking, 'Is it one of those tents where you don't have to use pegs?'

Halfway down the next incline a thought suddenly occurs to the boy. He slows briefly, arrested. 'Dad, hey, do you think that horse wanted something to eat?'

'Maybe,' says the man, cheerfully, dismissively, having to call because the boy has fallen behind.

The boy puts his concentration into keeping abreast.

Ten minutes later, when the ponies reach the brow, heading in for the night, there is no sign on the plain of the man and the boy. Too purposeful to loiter, too focused on their goal to stop and gaze at the still black mirror of lake, man and boy have crossed the tract of land and are gone.

They camp under the highest peak, on the far side of the plain. They have pitched their tent, they have lit their stove, and in the quick-dropping dark at the foot of the mountain they have eaten their reconstituted soup. And all the time the boy talked: about the stove, about the valve at the top of its canister of gas – gabbling, his voice growing shrill when the man failed to light it first time and the flare sputtered and died.

In the plummeting darkness, the man's own anxiety began to mount. He could feel it gathering in the blackening chill: the aching certainty that already, only one year on from the separation, he has lost his son, his child. And the thought grew so strong that he could only half-listen to the child's earnest desperate voice.

At last the child, tucked up in his sleeping-bag, chattered himself out.

The man gently takes away the torch.

It isn't long before the man, already expert at blanking out pain, falls asleep too.

Neither hears the horses moving round the tent in the night.

For years to come, though, in his dreams the boy will see their wild fringed eyes and feel the deep thudding of their hooves.

Further reading

Elizabeth Baines has recently published her first collection of short stories, *Balancing on the Edge of the World* (Salt Publishing, 2007), containing stories about the power struggles of children and adults.

An Ideal Family

by Katherine Mansfield

> Katherine Mansfield is considered one of the greatest short story writers of the 20th century. *An Ideal Family* comes from a collection called *The Garden Party and Other Stories* (Penguin Classics, 2007). Her stories focus on mood rather than plot. They describe the quite trivial events which can trigger subtle changes in human behaviour.

That evening for the first time in his life, as he pressed through the swing door and descended the three broad steps to the pavement, old Mr Neave felt he was too old for the spring. Spring – warm, eager, restless – was there, waiting for him in the golden light, ready in front of everybody to run up, to blow in his white beard, to drag sweetly on his arm. And he couldn't meet her, no; he couldn't square up once more and stride off, jaunty as a young man. He was tired and, although the late sun was still shining, curiously cold, with a numbed feeling all over. Quite suddenly he hadn't the energy, he hadn't the heart to stand this gaiety and bright movement any longer; it confused him. He wanted to stand still, to wave it away with his stick, to say, 'Be off with you!' Suddenly it was a terrible effort to greet as usual – tipping his wideawake[1] with his stick – all the people whom he knew, the friends, acquaintances, shopkeepers, postmen, drivers. But the gay glance that went with the gesture, the kindly twinkle that seemed to say, 'I'm a match and more for any of you' – that old Mr Neave could not manage at all. He stumped along, lifting his knees high as if he were walking through air that had somehow grown heavy and solid like water. And the homeward-looking crowd hurried by, the trams clanked, the light carts clattered, the big swinging cabs bowled along with

---

[1] **wideawake**   felt hat with a wide brim

that reckless, defiant indifference that one knows only in dreams...

It had been a day like other days at the office. Nothing special had happened. Harold hadn't come back from lunch until close on four. Where had he been? What had he been up to? He wasn't going to let his father know. Old Mr Neave had happened to be in the vestibule, saying good-bye to a caller, when Harold sauntered in, perfectly turned out as usual, cool, suave, smiling that peculiar little half-smile that women found so fascinating.

Ah, Harold was too handsome, too handsome by far; that had been the trouble all along. No man had a right to such eyes, such lashes, and such lips; it was uncanny. As for his mother, his sisters, and the servants, it was not too much to say they made a young god of him; they worshipped Harold, they forgave him everything; and he had needed some forgiving ever since the time when he was thirteen and he had stolen his mother's purse, taken the money, and hidden the purse in the cook's bedroom. Old Mr Neave struck sharply with his stick upon the pavement edge. But it wasn't only his family who spoiled Harold, he reflected, it was everybody; he had only to look and to smile, and down they went before him. So perhaps it wasn't to be wondered at that he expected the office to carry on the tradition. H'm, h'm! But it couldn't be done. No business – not even a successful, established, big paying concern – could be played with. A man had either to put his whole heart and soul into it, or it went all to pieces before his eyes...

And then Charlotte and the girls were always at him to make the whole thing over to Harold, to retire, and to spend his time enjoying himself. Enjoying himself! Old Mr Neave stopped dead under a group of ancient cabbage palms outside the Government buildings! Enjoying himself! The wind of evening shook the dark leaves to a thin airy cackle. Sitting at home, twiddling his thumbs, conscious all the while that his life's work was slipping away, dissolving, disappearing through Harold's fine fingers, while Harold smiled...

'Why will you be so unreasonable, father? There's absolutely no need for you to go to the office. It only makes it very awkward for us when people persist in saying how tired you're looking. Here's this huge house and garden. Surely you could be happy in – in – appreciating it for a change. Or you could take up some hobby.'

And Lola the baby had chimed in loftily, 'All men ought to have hobbies. It makes life impossible if they haven't.'

Well, well! He couldn't help a grim smile as painfully he began to climb the hill that led into Harcourt Avenue. Where would Lola and her sisters and Charlotte be if he'd gone in for hobbies, he'd like to know? Hobbies couldn't pay for the town house and the seaside bungalow, and their horses, and their golf, and the sixty-guinea gramophone in the music-room for them to dance to. Not that he grudged them these things. No, they were smart, good-looking girls, and Charlotte was a remarkable woman; it was natural for them to be in the swim. As a matter of fact, no other house in the town was as popular as theirs; no other family entertained so much. And how many times old Mr Neave, pushing the cigar box across the smoking-room table, had listened to praises of his wife, his girls, of himself even.

'You're an ideal family, sir, an ideal family. It's like something one reads about or sees on the stage.'

'That's all right, my boy,' old Mr Neave would reply. 'Try one of those; I think you'll like them. And if you care to smoke in the garden, you'll find the girls on the lawn, I dare say.'

That was why the girls had never married, so people said. They could have married anybody. But they had too good a time at home. They were too happy together, the girls and Charlotte. H'm, h'm! Well, well. Perhaps so . . .

By this time he had walked the length of fashionable Harcourt Avenue; he had reached the corner house, their house. The carriage gates were pushed back; there were fresh marks of wheels on the drive. And then he faced the big white-painted house, with its wide-open windows, its tulle curtains floating outwards, its blue jars of hyacinths on the broad sills. On either side of the carriage porch their hydrangeas – famous in the town – were coming into flower; the pinkish, bluish masses of flower lay like light among the spreading leaves. And somehow, it seemed to old Mr Neave that the house and the flowers, and even the fresh marks on the drive, were saying, 'There is young life here. There are girls – '

The hall, as always, was dusky with wraps, parasols, gloves, piled on the oak chests. From the music-room sounded the piano, quick, loud and impatient. Through the drawing-room door that was ajar voices floated.

'And were there ices?' came from Charlotte. Then the creak, creak of her rocker.

'Ices!' cried Ethel. 'My dear mother, you never saw such ices. Only two kinds. And one a common little strawberry shop ice, in a sopping wet frill.'

'The food altogether was too appalling,' came from Marion.

'Still, it's rather early for ices,' said Charlotte easily.

'But why, if one has them at all . . . ' began Ethel.

'Oh, quite so, darling,' crooned Charlotte.

Suddenly the music-room door opened and Lola dashed out. She started, she nearly screamed, at the sight of old Mr Neave.

'Gracious, father! What a fright you gave me! Have you just come home? Why isn't Charles here to help you off with your coat?'

Her cheeks were crimson from playing, her eyes glittered, the hair fell over her forehead. And she breathed as though she had come running through the dark and was frightened. Old Mr Neave stared at his youngest daughter; he felt he had never seen her before. So that was Lola, was it? But she seemed to have forgotten her father; it was not for him that she was waiting there. Now she put the tip of her crumpled handkerchief between her teeth and tugged at it angrily. The telephone rang.

A drawing room, circa 1920.

A-ah! Lola gave a cry like a sob and dashed past him. The door of the telephone-room slammed, and at the same moment Charlotte called, 'Is that you, father?'

'You're tired again,' said Charlotte reproachfully, and she stopped the rocker and offered her warm plum-like cheek. Bright-haired Ethel pecked his beard, Marion's lips brushed his ear.

'Did you walk back, father?' asked Charlotte.

'Yes, I walked home,' said old Mr Neave, and he sank into one of the immense drawing-room chairs.

'But why didn't you take a cab?' said Ethel. 'There are hundreds of cabs about at that time.'

'My dear Ethel,' cried Marion, 'if father prefers to tire himself out, I really don't see what business of ours it is to interfere.'

'Children, children?' coaxed Charlotte.

But Marion wouldn't be stopped. 'No, mother, you spoil father, and it's not right. You ought to be stricter with him. He's very naughty.' She laughed her hard, bright laugh and patted her hair in a mirror. Strange! When she was a little girl she had such a soft, hesitating voice; she had even stuttered, and now, whatever she said – even if it was only 'Jam, please, father' – it rang out as though she were on the stage.

'Did Harold leave the office before you, dear?' asked Charlotte, beginning to rock again.

'I'm not sure,' said old Mr Neave. 'I'm not sure. I didn't see him after four o'clock.'

'He said – ' began Charlotte.

But at that moment Ethel, who was twitching over the leaves of some paper or other, ran to her mother and sank down beside her chair.

'There, you see,' she cried. 'That's what I mean, mummy. Yellow, with touches of silver. Don't you agree?'

'Give it to me, love,' said Charlotte. She fumbled for her tortoise-shell spectacles and put them on, gave the page a little dab with her plump small fingers, and pursed up her lips. 'Very sweet!' she crooned vaguely; she looked at Ethel over her spectacles. 'But I shouldn't have the train.'

'Not the train!' wailed Ethel tragically. 'But the train's the whole point.'

'Here, mother, let me decide.' Marion snatched the paper playfully from Charlotte. 'I agree with mother,' she cried triumphantly. 'The train overweights it.'

Old Mr Neave, forgotten, sank into the broad lap of his chair, and, dozing, heard them as though he dreamed. There was no doubt about it, he was tired out; he had lost his hold. Even Charlotte and the girls were too much for him to-night. They were too ... too ... But all his drowsing brain could think of was – too rich for him. And somewhere at the back of everything he was watching a little withered ancient man climbing up endless flights of stairs. Who was he?

'I shan't dress to-night,' he muttered.

'What do you say, father?'

'Eh, what, what?' Old Mr Neave woke with a start and stared across at them. 'I shan't dress to-night,' he repeated.

'But, father, we've got Lucile coming, and Henry Davenport, and Mrs Teddie Walker.'

'It will look so very out of the picture.'

'Don't you feel well, dear?'

'You needn't make any effort. What is Charles for?'

'But if you're really not up to it,' Charlotte wavered.

'Very well! Very well!' Old Mr Neave got up and went to join that little old climbing fellow just as far as his dressing-room . . .

There young Charles was waiting for him. Carefully, as though everything depended on it, he was tucking a towel round the hot-water can. Young Charles had been a favourite of his ever since as a little red-faced boy he had come into the house to look after the fires. Old Mr Neave lowered himself into the cane lounge by the window, stretched out his legs, and made his little evening joke, 'Dress him up, Charles!' And Charles, breathing intensely and frowning, bent forward to take the pin out of his tie.

H'm, h'm! Well, well! It was pleasant by the open window, very pleasant – a fine mild evening. They were cutting the grass on the tennis court below; he heard the soft churr of the mower. Soon the girls would begin their tennis parties again. And at the thought he seemed to hear Marion's voice ring out, 'Good for you, partner . . . Oh, played, partner . . . Oh, very nice indeed.' Then Charlotte calling from the veranda, 'Where is Harold?' And Ethel, 'He's certainly not here, mother.' And Charlotte's vague, 'He said – '

Old Mr Neave sighed, got up, and putting one hand under his beard, he took the comb from young Charles, and carefully combed the white beard over. Charles gave him a folded hand-kerchief, his watch and seals,[2] and spectacle case.

---

[2] **seals**   signet rings, historically used to press a family crest or other symbol into sealing wax

'That will do, my lad.' The door shut, he sank back, he was alone ... And now that little ancient fellow was climbing down endless flights that led to a glittering, gay dining-room. What legs he had! They were like a spider's – thin, withered.

'You're an ideal family, sir, an ideal family.'

But if that were true, why didn't Charlotte or the girls stop him? Why was he all alone, climbing up and down? Where was Harold? Ah, it was no good expecting anything from Harold. Down, down went the little old spider, and then, to his horror, old Mr Neave saw him slip past the dining-room and make for the porch, the dark drive, the carriage gates, the office. Stop him, stop him, somebody!

Old Mr Neave started up. It was dark in his dressing-room; the window shone pale. How long had he been asleep? He listened, and through the big, airy, darkened house there floated far-away voices, far-away sounds. Perhaps, he thought vaguely, he had been asleep for a long time. He'd been forgotten. What had all this to do with him – this house and Charlotte, the girls and Harold – what did he know about them? They were strangers to him. Life had passed him by. Charlotte was not his wife. His wife!

... A dark porch, half hidden by a passion-vine, that drooped sorrowful, mournful, as though it understood. Small, warm arms were round his neck. A face, little and pale, lifted to his, and a voice breathed, 'Good-bye, my treasure.'

My treasure! 'Good-bye, my treasure!' Which of them had spoken? Why had they said good-bye? There had been some terrible mistake. She was his wife, that little pale girl, and all the rest of his life had been a dream.

Then the door opened, and young Charles, standing in the light, put his hands by his side and shouted like a young soldier, 'Dinner is on the table, sir!'

'I'm coming, I'm coming,' said old Mr Neave.

Further reading

Another of Katherine Mansfield's collections that you might enjoy is *Bliss* (Wordsworth Editions Ltd, 1999). Mansfield wrote a lot about her childhood. However, she was a member of the Bloomsbury Group of writers, which included Virginia Woolf and D. H. Lawrence – two famous authors whose works were mainly about adult life.

Activities

Lost and Found

Before you read

1 What do you know about the Vietnam war of the 1970s? Have you seen more recent stories on the news about children from war-torn countries being adopted by Westerners? What do you think might be some of the advantages and disadvantages for those children? Share what you know in a small group.

What's it about?

Read the text and answer questions 2 and 3 by yourself. Then compare your answers with a partner's.

2 Draw a simple timeline or 'story map' to show the main events in Sang's life so far. How does it compare with your own life?

3 How did Sang's babyhood differ from more fortunate children's? Make a list of negative words and phrases used in the text to describe it. What effect did these experiences have on his development?

Thinking about the text

4 Anderson says that Sang has lost 'everything in the world, including his own country'. Write a paragraph or two explaining what sort of effect you imagine losing his country would have on Sang. Will he recover from the damage it did? For your answer, think about the life he led before and the adjustments he had to make to adapt to his strange new life in England.

5 Imagine you are Sang's new head teacher in England. Write his school report describing his progress.

6 Look closely at the techniques the writer uses to engage our sympathy. Pick out three details that particularly strike you and analyse their effect. Write a short paragraph about each of your chosen examples. Think about:
- use of short simple sentences
- repeated words or lists ('no . . . no . . . no'; 'And . . . And . . . And')
- tiny details (e.g. the wicker chair, the red wooden brick)
- understatement
- contrast in the opening sentence.

A Family Photo, Two of Everything, Saturday Fathers and *New Families: the Experience of Divorce*

Before you read

1 The title of the first poem is *A Family Photo*. Sketch and label a picture of your own family. Would you need more than one group in your picture?

What's it about?

Read all four texts and answer questions 2 and 3 by yourself. Then compare your answers with a partner's.

2 Write down what Carla in *Two of Everything* means when she says 'there are two of me'. Then look at the comments in *New Families* and sum up the main problems of living in two homes mentioned by the children. Finally, write a sentence or two explaining the last line of *A Family Photo*.

3 Why is the lyric called *Saturday Fathers*? List four disadvantages of being a 'Saturday father'.

Thinking about the text

4 Imagine a child with two homes. Using the material in the texts to help you, write two short paragraphs describing some of the changes the child experiences when they move from one to the other. In what ways might they have to be two people?

5 In a small group, look closely at the language in *Saturday Fathers*. Explain in your own words what you understand by the following lines, and comment on their effect on the reader.
- ... *not above bribery / Spoiling that little too much*
- *Glamorous and generous and free*
- *Sweaty in yesterday's shirt*
- *The dads who must make do with courtesy*

6 Improvise a telephone conversation between a 'Saturday father' and his children during the week. Think about how awkward it might be on both sides.

The Ultimate Safari

Before you read

1 What would you find most frightening about being a refugee? Which home comforts would you find it hardest to do without? Discuss your thoughts with a partner.

What's it about?

Read the story and answer questions 2 to 4 by yourself. Then compare your answers with a partner's.

2 Why were the children pleased when their grandmother decided to leave the village? Why do you think the grandfather was less happy about it?

3 What skills and strengths helped this family to survive when so many others died?

4 At the end of the story, why do you think the grandmother doesn't want to answer the interviewer's question about going home?

Thinking about the text

5 Why do you think the writer chose the title *The Ultimate Safari*? Draw a spider diagram to show what you normally associate with a safari.

6 The story conveys very powerfully the confusion for the children, the bewildering events, the sounds and smells. List three descriptions which work particularly well in helping you to imagine what it would have been like. Give reasons for your choice.

7 What do you think was going through the grandmother's mind when she had to choose between saving the children and looking for her husband? Write a 'stream of consciousness' which describes her inner thoughts and feelings.

8 The children's grandmother was clearly a remarkable woman. Imagine that you are the girl in the story. Write a letter to your grandmother, thanking her for saving your life. Think about:
- what you, a child, might particularly remember of the journey
- what sacrifices the grandmother made.

Me, a Mother at 15? No Way! and The Sorrows of Sandra Saint

Before you read

1 How would having a baby change your life now? In a small group, discuss some of the problems that a pregnant 14-year-old is likely to face. What advice would you give her?

What's it about?

Read the texts and answer questions 2 to 4 by yourself. Then compare your answers with a partner's.

2 Sum up the theme of *Me, a Mother at 15* in two sentences.

3 In *The Sorrows of Sandra Saint*, how was Sandra's father killed? How do the three characters react to his death?

4 How does the advice in the book Sandra is reading contrast with her own circumstances? Is it useful to her? Would any information in *Me, a Mother at 15* help her? Explain your opinion with references to the texts.

Thinking about the text

5 In his introduction to a collection of his plays, Lee Hall says: 'All the plays attempt to weave pathos and humour inseparably.' Do you think he has achieved this in *The Sorrows of Sandra Saint*? Discuss your thoughts with a partner, looking for examples of both qualities in the text and examining the effect on the reader of the words and phrases Hall chooses.

6 Prepare a talk for your class on the problem of teenage pregnancy, using information from both texts and any other sources you can find, such as the website http://www.stayteen.org

7 'Focus One . . . has no plans to let the baby loose on boys.' Do you think boys should have the same experience as the girls in *Me, a Mother at 15*? Have a debate in a small group.

8 Write a comparison of the two very different pieces. The first uses journalistic techniques and describes real people, the second uses the techniques of dramatic dialogue and characterisation. Which one has the most effect on you, and why? Would either piece influence your behaviour by making you 'more careful'?

Compass and Torch

Before you read

1 Can you remember any special trips with one of your parents? Think about the feelings you had – maybe a mixture of excitement and anxiety, or huge anticipation that fell a bit flat. Make brief notes and share them with a partner.

What's it about?

Read the story and answer questions 2 to 4 by yourself. Then compare your answers with a partner's.

2 Draw two columns. In one column, write down any words and phrases that convey the boy's anxiety. In the other, collect evidence of his excitement. Have you and your partner chosen the same words and phrases?

3 Why is the boy's mother worried about the trip? What might influence her feelings?

4 What kind of relationship does the boy have with Jim? How does it compare with the relationship with his dad?

Thinking about the text

5 How does the writer use the setting to add to the tension? What do the ponies add to the story? Would it make any difference if they weren't there? Write a short piece describing the effect of the setting on you, the reader, quoting from the text to support your points.

6 What do you think the father feels about the trip? Write his inner thoughts as a monologue.

7 What do you think the boy will tell his mother and her boyfriend about the trip with his father? Write or improvise another scene.

An Ideal Family

Before you read

1 What's the recipe for an 'ideal family'? Make a list of ingredients with a partner. You could refer to Sue Palmer's piece, *Forging a Family* (pages 29-32), to help you.

2 In a small group, share what you know (from films, TV or your reading) about life in a well-to-do family a hundred years ago. Think particularly about the roles of men and women.

What's it about?

Read the story and answer questions 3 to 5 by yourself. Then compare your answers with a partner's.

3 What clues can you find to the date of this story? What social attitudes have changed since then?

4 What do you think are the factors that contribute to Mr Neave feeling 'too old for the spring'? Is his family 'ideal'? If not, what has gone wrong?

5 What is it about Harold's character that worries his father? How do you think he will measure up to the job of running the business? Is Mr Neave right to worry?

Thinking about the text

6 The story is told entirely from Mr Neave's point of view. Look closely at how the writer helps us to identify with him physically as well as emotionally, and to imagine what it feels like to be old. Write a short essay about how she achieves this, picking out details from the text to illustrate each point.

7 Write a description of the 'ideal family' seen through the eyes of one of the children. Try and include period details to make it as authentic as you can.

8 Is it inevitable that older members of the family are sidelined by the young? What is your own experience? Discuss your ideas in a small group.

Compare and contrast

1 *Lost and Found* and *The Ultimate Safari* both deal with the issue of refugees and the confusion they experience when they lose their home. The outcomes for the two children in the stories are very different. How did they react? Do you think they suffered an equal loss of identity? Write a short essay comparing the two pieces, justifying your opinions by quoting from the texts.

2 The two poems *A Family Photo* and *Two of Everything* and the lyric *Saturday Fathers* are all concerned with divorce and separation. Write a short review comparing and contrasting the three texts. Think about:
- the verse form, including rhyme patterns if any
- point of view – who is speaking?
- use of imagery
- style and mood
- which had the most impact on you, and why.

3 Re-read *Saturday Fathers* and *Compass and Torch* and make some notes comparing the information given in each text about the experience of being a single father. Then plan and perform an improvisation portraying a group of fathers who aren't living with their children any more. Imagine, for instance, that they are talking in the pub about their experiences. You could develop this further by turning it into a radio play.

4 Write a short essay comparing the three short stories *The Ultimate Safari*, *Compass and Torch* and *An Ideal Family*. Think about:
- how the writers use the setting to create atmosphere
- how they help us to identify with the characters
- how they build tension
- the effect of the story openings and endings.

4 History and continuity

I am the family face.

This section broadens the theme of family life to consider its changing patterns over the centuries. Somebody from Victorian times, when children where expected to be 'seen but not heard', would probably be shocked at the relationship between parents and children today. But there are elements that stay the same. Most of you will recognise some aspects of your own family where life carries on in the same way from one generation to the next – maybe special ways of doing things, or the treasuring of precious possessions that once belonged to a grandparent.

Activities

1 How much do you know about your own family history? And who do you 'take after'? Prepare a short talk.

2 Some families keep in close touch with grandparents and other relatives. Others rarely see them. Think of some of the reasons for this, and then discuss the advantages and disadvantages of close or distant family networks.

3 Do you value tradition, or do you favour the future? Have a class debate.

Two poems
by Judith Nicholls

Judith Nicholls wrote her first poem when she was seven! She believes that 'anyone can write a poem . . . as long as they are happy to keep "twiddling" with it until it really says what they want to say and how!'

She is now one of Britain's best-known poets for young people. Her poems are simple and direct but say a lot.

Beginnings

In the beginning
was one.
Crouched in a cave
where bats first hung,
where webs were first woven,
dreams first spun,
crouched one,
alone.

And then one day
into the gloom
another came;
the fire was lit
the cave was warmed,
the howl of the wind
became a song
and two
were one.

Soon winter passed,
and into the sun
from the dark of the cave
one summer dawn

crept three:
the third was a child in arms,
the three were
    a family, new-born.

A family tree.

Family Tree

I am
the family tree.
Before time barely had begun
I rooted,
splintering frozen stone.

I am
the family tree.
Through fire and ice I've crept and crawled,
roots stretching wider,
branches tall.

I am
the family tree.
Those roots, now laced in ancient moss,
still feed young branches
grasping into space.

I am their base;
I am your base.

Further reading

Judith Nicholls has edited several poetry anthologies as well as publishing her own collections. You might enjoy *Earthways, Earthwise* (Oxford University Press, 1993), an anthology about conservation.

You can hear her reading her poems at http://www.poetryarchive.org

From the Grave to the Cradle
by Hugh Cunningham

> *The Invention of Childhood* is a book, based on a BBC Radio Four series, which traces the history of childhood and family life; it covers over a thousand years. This extract tells of the very beginning of that time, before there were written records.

Grave number 133 in the seventh-century Anglo-Saxon cemetery at Castledyke South, Barton-on-Humber, is less than a metre in length. That is one reason why we know that an infant was buried there. There is another reason. The bones have crumbled away, but, as was the norm for the pagan[1] Anglo-Saxons before the coming of Christianity, the infant was buried with objects associated with it. In the grave, alongside three glass beads, was a feeding bottle, shaped like a breast. Perhaps the mother had not been able to produce any milk. Perhaps, as other Anglo-Saxon graves tell us, the baby had a cleft palate[2] and could not suckle. Whatever the reason, the bottle is evidence of a vain attempt to sustain life in a baby, of parental care for a child. That parental care, set alongside its opposite, parental neglect or cruelty, will run through this history of children in Britain.

So too will another message we can take from the grave. Parents all too often had to come to terms with the deaths of their children. We have no figures for death rates of children in the early Middle Ages, but there is no reason to suppose they were any better than in later centuries when probably at least one out of every four babies born would fail to live to their first birthday. If you survived your first hours, days, weeks and months of life, your prospects improved, but perhaps as many as a half of all children born would fail to reach the age of ten.

---

[1] **pagan**   someone without a religion
[2] **cleft palate**   a split in the roof of the mouth

When we look at the history of childhood we are constantly confronted with parents trying to cope with the deaths of their children, and children facing the possibility of their own deaths or those of their siblings . . .

And of course it was not only children who died. Parents died too. The rate of break-up of the family through parental death in all centuries up to the twentieth century was roughly equivalent to our twenty-first-century rate of break-up through divorce. The death of a parent meant that many children were brought up by one parent alone or had to adjust to a step-parent; or the loss of both parents meant that some other means of care had to be found.

The infant's grave has one further message. Historians of childhood, particularly in the early Middle Ages, have to exercise considerable ingenuity[3] in order to find out anything about children. There are all too many questions to which there is no answer. But sometimes the most unlikely material can at least give us clues. A survey of Anglo-Saxon burial places reveals that children under 15 constituted just over one-third of all burials, a lower percentage than one would expect. This may have been because children's corpses were disposed of in other ways, an indicator that their status[4] was lower than that of adults. Certainly children were less likely than adults to be buried with grave goods. These are clues, but archaeologists and historians are never likely to be in full agreement about their meaning.

---

[3]**ingenuity** cleverness
[4]**status** position in society

'Forget the wheel. Invent diapers.'

(www.CartoonStock.com)

Further reading

If you want to know more about children through the ages, *The Invention of Childhood* is available as a book (BBC Books, 2006) and as a CD (BBC Audiobooks Ltd, 2006). Hugh Cunningham has also written *Children and Childhood in Western Society since 1500* (Longman, 2005). Michael Morpurgo co-presented the radio series and his children's books are probably already known to you. One of his novels with a family theme, told through letters between a brother and sister, is *Dear Olly* (Collins, 2007).

Little Brother

by Mary Mann

> Imagine being so poor that your clothes were made of sacking . . . .
> Mary Mann's stories, written in Victorian times, paint a vivid picture
> of the desperate poverty amongst farm labourers in Norfolk. As a
> farmer's wife, she had first-hand knowledge of village life.

I met the parish nurse hurrying from the cottage in which a baby had, that morning, been born, towards a cottage at the other end of the village where a baby was due to be born, that night.

'All well over!' she said. 'Mrs Hodd going on nicely as can be expected.'

'She ought to be used to it by now, Nurse! The thirteenth!'

'Well, this one is dead. Born dead.'

'What a mercy!'

But our nurse does not like a case where the baby is born dead. 'Such a beautiful child too!'

'It's more than can be said of the other twelve.'

'How can you tell?' Nurse said. 'Look at their clothes; look at their hair, standing on end; look at the scenes they live in!'

'The Hodds ought to be sent to prison for having thirteen children.'

'Go and tell Hodd himself so. You'll find him, if you go through the farm-yard. In the turnip-house. He slept there, last night; did not come home at all. He always clears out on these occasions. "A good riddance," Mrs Hodd says.'

Mr Hodd answered my greeting by a side-ways chuck of his head, and went on turning the handle of the cutting-machine which a small boy, working with him, replenished with whole turnips. The father of thirteen was a wild, unkempt-looking creature, habited in an outer garment composed of a dirty sack, through the hole cut in the bottom of which his head projected; a tangle of matted red hair met a tangle of matted red beard; a small portion of white cheek beneath the angry-looking blue eyes was the only part of his face uncovered. His arms, thrust through the slits cut in the sides of the sack, were hung about with rags which might once have been sleeves of a grey flannel shirt. Not such a family as the Hodds do we often see in Dulditch, but in the present shortage of labour the farmers are glad to welcome what help they can get.

'So I hear your wife's given birth to a dead baby, Hodd.'

Swish – swish – swish went the knife through the turnips, the neat sections dropping into the basket beneath. Two revolutions of the handle, then a curt, 'So they tell me.'

'Haven't you been home to see your wife?'

'No.' Swish – swish. 'Nor ain't a-goin'.'

'I think you ought to go. Mrs Hodd will be wanting to see you.'

Two vicious turns of the handle of the machine which the boy feeds assiduously. Hodd is 'putting his back into it,' this morning!

'She's borne you many children, Hodd.'

'A sight too many!' Swish – swish. 'The place is chuck full of 'em. You stamp on 'em as you walk.'

'They keep you poor, I'm afraid!'

'Ah!' Swish – swish – swish.

'At any rate this poor little one won't have to be fed; you're no worse off than before it came.'

'There'll soon be another,' Hodd grunted, savagely prophetic. 'There's no stoppin' my missus, once she' got a-goin'.'

The reflection that it was hardly fair to put it all on to Mrs Hodd, this way, I kept to myself.

The little boy, pitching the turnips into the voracious maw of the machine, looked at me brightly. He also was redheaded, he also was attired for the most part in a sack. He was the eldest hope of the Hodd family, helping his father in the hour between morning and afternoon school.

'Him and me – ,' a nod in the direction of his parent, 'have got to make a box tonight, when we laves off wark,' he said. 'Mother, she've sent ward by Nurse we've got to make a box to put little brother in.'

'Ah, poor little one!'

'Then him and me,' a chuck of his chin at the parent Hodd, 'is a-goin' to carry 'm to the corner of the chech-yard where there ain't no blessin'.'[1]

'Now then! Git on wi' them turmits, boy.' In his pleasurable anticipation of the jaunt before him, the boy had stopped in his work. But he at once re-addressed himself to the task of throwing the turnips into the ever-open mouth of the cutter, where they bobbed about merrily for a moment or two before settling into position for the knives to slice.

'Well, good morning, Hodd,' I said. 'I shall go to see your wife and the poor baby before it is put in the box.'

Swish. Swish. Swish.

In the kitchen I passed through on my way upstairs, a pair of Hodds, of too tender an age to be at school, were seated on a sack – again a sack! – spread before the fire, and were playing with a large battered doll. Mrs Hodd, above, lay in her big squalid bed, alone.

'Have you no one to wait on you?'

'Blesh you, yes! There's the gal Maude.' Maude was the twelve years old daughter. 'Nonly she've gone on a narrand now, to let the parson's[2] folk know as I'm brought to bed, and to ask for a drop o' soup, and a packet o' gro'ts, and a few nouraging matters o' that sort. For I've got to have life kep' in me somehow, I s'pose. And if parson's folk don't do it I don't know who should.'

'So the poor baby is dead, this time, Mrs Hodd!'

---

[1] **the corner of the chech-yard where there ain't no blessin'** the unconsecrated (not declared holy) part of the churchyard

[2] **parson** priest, minister of the church

Mrs Hodd wrung her nose round to the middle of her cheek with a loud snuffle, tears streamed from her blue eyes. (All the Hodd family have red hair and blue eyes; so adorned themselves, and having started on a family thus endowed,[3] Mr and Mrs Hodd had never paused to alter the pattern.)

'That fare hard,' she gurgled, 'to go t'rough it all, and then to lose 'em.'

'But you have so many, Mrs Hodd. This little one could well be spared. Hodd thinks as I do.'

'Ah! Hodd, he han't a mother's heart!'

'I am sure it is all you can do to feed and clothe the twelve.'

'Clothe? I don't clothe 'em. I look after their insides. No one can't say as my child'en look starved. If parson's folk want to see 'em clothed they must do it theirselves. My job's their insides, I take it.'

---

[3]**endowed** equipped

'I should like to see the poor baby, Mrs Hodd. I hear it was a very fine child.'

'Mine allers is!' Mrs Hodd testified. 'A crop o' heer he'd got all over his poll like golden suverins.[4] My little uns, they're all that plased wi' their little brother! A fine hollerin' there'll be when he's took off to the buryin'.'

'Where is he? Look, I've brought a few flowers to lay upon his tiny coffin.'

Mrs Hodd, without lifting her tousled head, cast a glance of enquiry round the almost bare room. Near the door a rude bed had been made by spreading a towel over a frowsy pillow laid on two chairs.

'Ain't he theer?' the woman asked, her eyes upon the chairs.

'Nothing's there, Mrs Hodd.'

'Randolph!' Mrs Hodd screamed with startling abruptness. ' 'Vangeline! Come you here, this minute; don't I'll warm yer jackets for ye when I git yer.'

'Pray do not excite yourself,' I cried, alarmed. 'If you want the children who are in the kitchen I will fetch them for you.'

The tiny children on the filthy hearth were too much engrossed with their play to be aware of me, standing to watch. They were striving to draw over the rigid legs of the doll the grey calico[5] nightgown of which they were stripping it when I saw them last. Their fat dirty little hands trembled with their eagerness to accomplish this feat. The mite who had the toy on her knees rocked herself maternally, and gave chirrups of encouragement as she worked.

'Theer! put ickle arms in! Put in ickle arms!'

Failing in every effort to insert the arms, she decided to dispense with that formality; pulling the awful nightgown over the shoulders she knotted it at the back of a little red head.

---

[4] **suverins** gold sovereigns (old coins)
[5] **calico** tough cotton cloth

Then she turned the battered doll on its back and I saw that it was the dead baby.

Evangeline and Randolph pushed their grubby fingers into the open mouth, and tried to force them into the sunken eyes, in order to raise the lids.

'Wake up! Wake up, ickle brudder!' they said.

When I had rescued the desecrated[6] body, and borne it to its poor bier[7] in the mother's room, I spoke a word to Mrs Hodd which she resented.

'Time is long for sech little uns, when t'others 're at school and I'm laid by,' she said. 'Other folkes' child'en have a toy, now and then, to kape 'em out o' mischief. My little uns han't. He've kep' 'em quite[8] for hours, the po'r baby have; and I'll lay a crown they han't done no harm to their little brother.'

Further reading

Tales of Victorian Norfolk (Morrow & Co, 1998) was rediscovered and broadcast on BBC Radio in 2008. The stories are sometimes grim but humorous too. If you are interested in reading more about the lives of the Victorian poor, try Henry Mayhew's *London Street Life* (Chatto Education, 1966).

---

[6]**desecrated** treated with contempt
[7]**bier** stand for laying out a body prior to burial
[8]**quite** quiet, pronounced in Mrs Hodd's accent

Keeping Mum

by Sara Selvarajah

> *In Your Own Words* is a collection of family memories – 'extraordinary tales from ordinary life' – submitted by readers to the *Sunday Telegraph Magazine*. This extract comes from a section on parenthood.

If you had met my father hovering in the Stanley Gibbons shop on the Strand, or battling up the hill to my house laden down with orange plastic bags stretched taut over the newly acquired first-day cover albums,[1] you would have thought him just another almost-integrated Asian stamp-collector. His oversized car-coat was never quite right for the occasion and his thick-soled Bata shoes were the sort young boys were forced into by their mothers for the first day of junior school. He would arrive at my door, bags at his feet, propped up against the wall with one hand, inhaler in the other, barely able to speak, his airways constricted by the asthma attack brought on by exposure to the cool, damp English air, and the effort of his victory over the incline of my road. 'You should have phoned me from the station, Dad.'

'What for, when I can walk?' He did not know how to accept with grace – not a lift, not a gift, not a gesture. As children we treated him with varying degrees of caution, and as adults we found our own ways of communicating with him.

For my part, I learnt to gain his unreserved affection through academic success. From my earliest memories of him teaching me to count, and later to multiply, using burnt-out matchsticks which I stored in a wooden matchbox till the day I graduated, I felt his pride and approval. Maybe it was the old story of the first-generation immigrant seeking success for his offspring in the revered English educational system, or maybe

---

[1] **first-day cover albums** valuable collections of first-day-issued postage stamps

it was just the way we found to take pleasure from each other. But it was where we met and understood each other, until I found another place to meet him.

My third child was due in four days, and my parents had arrived in the morning to see my elder son, aged five, perform in a school play. It became evident during the performance that the contractions which I had been experiencing but ignoring for several hours were real, but, since they did not progress quickly and the play was almost over, I continued to ignore them. By the time we returned home I was in some pain and my father had noticed. 'Are you in labour? Do you know how dangerous this is, you silly girl? Call your husband and get to the hospital right now.'

I did as he said, accepting that a full-blown labour after two Caesarean sections was not recommended. But before I left I spoke to my son. 'Mummy's got to go to the hospital to have the baby. I won't be away too long, so be a good boy and look after your brother while I'm away.'

I turned to see my father sitting on the steps, his head in his hands. He couldn't explain why he was upset and I was ushered away to the hospital. I came home five days later with a new baby and my father wept. 'I remembered,' he said. 'After sixty years, I remembered. How my mother left me with my brother and used the same words as you used when you spoke to Joseph. But she never came back. The servant said, "Your mother is dead," and I didn't understand. He took me into a room and said, "This is your mother's body. After today you will never see her again. That's what it means to be dead." But you came home to your sons. I am so happy for them.'

Further reading

In Your Own Words (Pocket Books, 2006) is a good book for dipping into: all the stories are short; some are sad, some funny.

Oral Tradition

by Carolyn Steele Agosta

> The American family in this story carry on a tradition through generations: going to Camp Meeting. For two weeks every summer, they meet for worship, singing, socialising and family reunions. This year it's important for the old and the young.

Gramma fusses about getting ready for Camp Meeting this year, even though she has it organized down to the last baked bean and roll of toilet paper. She's been going every year since she was born, 1939, and so I guess she knows what's needed, but she really gets into the whole 'tradition' thing. I'll try to stick in something new, like my Walkman or Gameboy, and she just throws a hissy fit. 'That's not what Camp Meeting is about,' she says, packing her sun tea jar and a bag of lemons. 'It's about family, and Jesus, and knowing why the good Lord put us on earth. Now where did you put the Skip-Bo cards?'

I find the cards and the board for the marble game, give them to her and tiptoe away. Grampa is sleeping in the living room in his wheelchair with all the shades pulled and I lay on the floor in the half-darkness. The wide wood boards are cool, but hard, and I can feel my ribs and hipbones grinding against them...

When I think about it, I've been going to Camp Meeting every year since I was born, just like Gramma, but fourteen years just isn't the same as sixty-one. Grampa never went to Camp Meeting when he was young, the year he met Gramma was his very first time. And he was just visiting a friend. So you never can tell what might happen.

Mumma and Brian aren't staying overnight this year. Mumma says it's too hot for little Kinsey, that she would get heat rash. Gramma fusses about that, too. 'It's just for two weeks,' she grumbles. 'You'd think that for fourteen days out of the whole year, a person could go without their air conditioning. Lord knows, we all got along under more primitive conditions than this when I was a girl.' She adds lawn chairs ... to her list. 'We never get a chance to talk any more.'

Mumma and Brian just say they have to work and they'll come out in the evenings. I'll help Gramma hold down the fort. I don't mind being the only one. It's hard on her, I know, to be away from Grampa. They've never been apart before.

Gramma fusses heavily the day we move into the tent. She keeps checking her lists to make sure she has everything. It's a matter of pride with her not to have forgotten anything. We hook the big wooden swings to the rings in the porch ceiling and cover the bench with an old quilt. She has all these pictures on the wall in her spare room at home, showing the family on the porch of the tent over the years. I like the pictures from the fifties, where the girls are all wearing short shorts and cat's-eye sunglasses, and the ones from the seventies, where they all have halter tops and bell bottoms. Some of the pictures have twenty or more people in them. Now there are only the seven of us. Gramma fills up the empty places on the porch with potted geraniums and petunias. It's my job to water them each morning.

Aunt Jody brings Grampa out for a while every evening. She stays at the house with him at night and he goes to day care for old people during the day. It's almost like he and Kinsey are the same age nowadays. They both wear diapers and sleep a lot. Aunt Jody likes to sit on the swing and say hey to all her old boyfriends when they walk by with their wives ... 'Hey, Dwayne.' She smiles slowly, her lips with their shiny peach color sliding back over her square, white teeth. 'How y'all doin'?'

Dwayne (or Bill, or Travis, or Eddie) always smiles nervously. Aunt Jody hasn't changed much since the time when she posed for that centerfold and the wives always make angry faces when they see her sitting there in her short shorts and little cotton tops. She has real good legs for a woman over thirty, they're brown as peaches with little golden freckles on the thighs, and she likes to cross them real slow . . .

Gramma tries to talk Aunt Jody into taking a day off . . . 'Why?' Aunt Jody asks. 'You know we'll only end up fussing at each other.'

'We could talk about things.'

'No, Mama. We never talk. We just fuss.' Aunt Jody checks her hair in her compact mirror and winks at me. 'I'll come in the evenings, I'm on a low-fuss diet these days.'

During the day, most people have to go to work, and the only ones there are the old people and the kids. Gramma is always over at the canteen, helping to fix meals. I don't think they could even have Camp Meeting if she wasn't there to make hush puppies[1] and fried chicken and 'nanner pudding.[2] I hang out with my friend, Ashley, and help with the younger kids during Bible school. Not that anybody asked me if I minded doing it, somehow it's always just expected that the girls will help. Nobody expects it of the boys, which seems unfair to me. They just hang out at the creek all day long, fishing and sometimes skinny-dipping. One day, Ashley and I sneak off to watch them. Ashley says you can tell just by looking which ones will be successful in their later lives, but it makes me feel all fussed inside my chest to see them so I tell her I have to go help Gramma with the snapbeans . . .

It's hot, really hot, even at night and Gramma lets me sleep on the upstairs porch. It's not much cooler but I like to watch the whole place slowly settle down and go to sleep. Then it's just me and the crickets and moths and the stars. The moon rises right up over the arbor, it's the prettiest sight.

Sometimes the boys will gather, quietly, whispering and passing a cigarette, and walk through the campground. I lay still as can be, my face pressed into the pillow that still smells of

---

[1] **hush puppies**   fried cornbread
[2] **'nanner pudding**   banana pudding

Gramma's iron-on starch, and try to hear what they're saying. Boys fascinate me, I have to admit. They're so different from girls and get to do lots better things. I know all about how girls have more opportunity nowadays, Aunt Jody is always telling me that, but it still seems like boys have more interesting lives. The only thing Aunt Jody ever did interesting was when she posed for that centerfold, and Mumma has never done anything interesting at all. Grampa helped blast holes in the mountains for roads, and Brian is a volunteer fireman and even stupid Lonnie Sigmon down the road drives a dirtbike in motor-cross races. The most exciting thing I ever did was ride the elephant when the Cole Brothers Circus had their show over at the elementary school. It's not a lot to look back on.

Each night the number of visitors grows. Ashley and I get dressed up in the evening after supper. She put a lot of Sun-In on her hair this summer and it really looks good. Mine is all curly from the humidity, so all I can do is stick it up in a big bushy ponytail. I finally got Mumma to let me wear mascara, though, so we both look lots older than last year. We walk round and round the campground, over and over, smiling at the boys and looking to see if they're smiling at us. Taylor Witherspoon has been looking at me a lot, which is good since he's one of the few boys taller than me. He's wearing glasses now and it makes him look real smart, and he has this sort of slow grin that just does something to me. We don't talk much, but one night we're both sitting on Ashley's porch and when he goes to stand up, he puts his hand on my shoulder first. It makes a little thrill run right down my arm and out at my elbow.

Friday night before Big Sunday, the crowds really get heavy. Gramma has been cooking all day at the canteen. 'It's too much,' Mumma fusses at her. 'You can't work all day in that hot kitchen, they shouldn't ask it.' Gramma's mouth makes a real straight line and she begins folding napkins and stomps around, putting the silverware straight. Mumma sighs and sits by Brian, who's pushing Kinsey back and forth in the stroller. Brian is always a little nervous around Gramma.

'Yes, Miz Abernathy,' he replies to everything she says. 'You're sure right about that.' I think Gramma just eats that up...

'The price of gas is something awful. I think the government should just put its foot down and refuse to have anything to do with those oil cartel countries. Don't you, Brian?'

'Yes, Miz Abernathy. It's a terrible thing, gas prices.'...

Jody brings Grampa in his wheelchair. Lots of people come by to say hey to him and Gramma sits next to him, her eyes sparkling. She talks and laughs and pats Grampa's hand. He smiles and taps his toe to the country music playing on the radio. Every time somebody new walks up, she tells him in his ear who it is. 'The Sherrills,' she says. 'You remember, Junior and Kat.'

'Junior and Kat,' he repeats, nodding and smiling. He enjoys the homemade strawberry ice cream. Gramma spoons it carefully into his mouth and kisses him on the cheek. 'Jenny?' he says loudly. 'Jenny. Jenny?'

'I'm right here, Frank.'

'Jenny! Where's Jenny?' he says loudly, and people across the way turn to look.

'Time to go home,' Jody says, and undoes the lock on his chair wheels. 'Mama, he gets worse every day, you've got to start giving some serious thought...'

'When I want your opinion, I'll ask for it, missy.'

'No, Jody's right,' Mumma insists. 'You have to face facts, Mama, you're not as young as you used to be and Daddy's a lot of work. You can't keep on lifting him and bathing him, you're going to hurt yourself one of these days. Now that he's adjusting to the daycare, you should consider...'

'Well, I'll be dipped in crumbs and fried in hell before I'll let one of my daughters tell me what I can and cannot do!' Gramma's eyes are blazing and her short, curly hair seems to be standing up on her head. I can see the glare of the setting sun behind it outlining her skull. 'We get along just fine, Frank and

I, and if I need help with him, I have plenty of friends who'd be glad to give a hand. *Glad* to. Don't you be worrying about us. Y'all just go back to your air-conditioned offices and busy, busy lives and let us take care of ourselves.' She glares at Mumma and walks over to Grampa, putting her hand on his shoulder.

'Jenny?' he says. 'Don't fuss. You're always fussing.' . . .

It rains that afternoon. I like rain at Camp Meeting. Gramma and I sit in the upper room and play cards to the sound of the rain hitting the tin roof. Little puffs of cool air slip in between the open slats of the wood walls. Gramma's hands shuffle the cards, her red fingernails flashing. I like to think about her being fourteen once, and playing cards with her Gramma during a warm July rain. 'Gin,' she says, and slaps down a fan of cards.

That night it's even hotter and we can hear thunder rolling up from the lake. It's gonna be a whopper of a storm, so Gramma and I take quilts and pillows and a flashlight out to her car, parked in the field beyond the furthest ring of tents. Gramma brings a jug of lemonade and some cookies, too. We nestle in the back seat, reading stuff from the National Enquirer to each other. Gramma keeps back issues in the car so she'll always have something to read when she's waiting at Grampa's doctor appointments. I like the ones with pictures of celebrity fashions, especially the ones showing the best-dressed and the worst-dressed. 'You'd think they could do better,' Gramma says, 'with all the money they make. Look at that girl, she has a perfect figure, a perfect face. Then she wears that tacky dress. She's just a mess. They had style, in my day.'

The rain begins really coming down, with flashes of lightning that make it like day and thunder that hurts your ears. I can see people in some of the other cars, their breath steaming up the windows. Gramma's perfume is stronger in this enclosed space. Avon's Topaze, which she has always worn till I can't think of anyone but her when I smell it.

'Grampa looked good tonight, didn't he,' she says, more of a statement than a question. I think about how it seems like he has no chest anymore, he is so curled over on himself. 'He liked the singing, I think.'

This seems almost like talking. I roll over on my back with my head in her lap and my knees pulled up. 'You met him here, didn't you?' I ask. I've heard the story a thousand times, but sometimes you just have to give a person their cue.

'He was visiting the Hendersons,' Gramma says, her eyes closed. 'He was just out of the service, almost 30 years old. I was only eighteen. He'd never seen a Camp Meeting before and they had to explain to him about why the cabins are called tents and suchlike. I was working at the canteen and he told Carl Henderson he'd never seen a woman with such a flat backside. I overheard him and said, quick as a shot, "that's because I don't waste time the good Lord gave me just sitting on it". He told me later it was what decided him to get to know me better. That I could give him a setdown like that without missing a beat.' She strokes my hair for a while and I watch raindrops chase each other down the back window. 'We were married before Christmas.' Lightning flashes again and I can see Gramma's red lipstick looking dark against her white skin. I roll on my side and mush my face into her stomach. The housedress she's wearing smells like sunshine and warm breezes. 'He was so good-looking,' she says. 'I thought he hung the moon.'

She looks down at me, sternly. 'Always set your standards high, girl. Don't date any stupid boys, you hear?'

I nod against her warm belly. 'Yes, ma'am. I mean, no, ma'am. I mean, I won't.'

'Your Grampa was a self-educated man, an intelligent man. He read everything he could get his hands on.' After a minute, she corrects herself. '*Is* a self-educated man.' Lightning flashes again, with thunder right on top of it and we both jump. 'Mercy,' she laughs. 'Good thing old Banjo isn't here, remember how afraid he used to be of storms? Used to whine and fuss until one of us would go sit with him in a dark closet.'

'I miss Banjo. He was a good ol' dog.' I loop my first finger around Gramma's belt, tug at it a little. 'I felt bad when he got old, he got so shaky and nervous. He shrank down to nothing.' I twine my other fingers in Gramma's belt, too, taking hold. 'Just like Grampa,' I whisper. 'He's disappearing bit by bit, like Banjo did.'

'Not quite like Banjo,' Gramma says, her voice quiet and tired-sounding. 'Banjo just wanted comforting when he got sick. You didn't need to worry about leaving him his dignity. You didn't need to . . .' She hushes up suddenly and looks out the window. Thunder booms real close by and the car shakes with it. She strokes my hair again. 'I know they want me to put him in a nursing home, but I just can't do it. I realize things are changing. I know they think I'm too old to take care of him but you don't just take the person you love and put them away! My mama and daddy lived in their own home right up until they died. People took care of each other in those days, that was what they *did*.'

'But I think that's what Mumma and Aunt Jody are trying to do for you, Gramma. They don't want to see you get sick too.'

'I'd rather they bury us together than split us up.'

Gramma's voice has that sound of finality, like when she told Aunt Jody that no way were they painting the house Wedgwood blue, it was going to stay white and green like it'd always been, and the thought of burying Gramma takes me so hard I almost start to bawl, my mouth wide open in a silent wail. I force tears and snot back where they belong and mush my face harder against her belly. Her hand curves over the back of my head and we struggle along for a few minutes, gulping and swallowing without saying a word.

The storm stops. As if it had wanted to go out with a bang, like 4th of July fireworks, it pounds out a final volley of thunder and lightning and then goes quietly away. Gramma pats my shoulder and I sit up, quickly wiping my face with the tail of my t-shirt. We gather our things and carry them back to the tent, dodging raindrops still dripping from the trees. The long wet grass catches at my ankles, soaking my sneakers and making them alternately stick and slide on the muddy clay soil. Even though it's after midnight, everyone's awake, talking and excited from the storm. Gramma picks up her pot of geraniums that had tipped over and presses the earth back down around their roots. 'You'll be fine,' she tells them. 'Sun'll be back tomorrow.'

Big Sunday brings the biggest crowds of all. Everyone dressed up in church clothes and carrying picnic lunches. Gramma goes all out, with slow-cooked barbecue, fresh-made slaw, silver queen corn on the cob. She doesn't have any truck with people who take the easy way out, bringing in tubs of KFC or cardboard boxes from the supermarket deli. 'I just don't understand how people can let all their traditions die out.' She puts her best tablecloth on the big rough table that Grampa built in the downstairs room a long time ago, and sets out real plates, not paper ones that can be thrown away afterward. Mumma has made lemon chess pies and Jody puts a jug of daisies in the middle of the table. Grampa is asleep in his wheelchair, but he wakes up when we're ready to eat. He still likes to eat Gramma's cooking, even if we have to cut it up real small. I take Kinsey out of the stroller. She's cutting teeth now and drools all over my good blouse. When she grins, all that spit makes a bubble. I get a slobbery kiss from her and sit down at the table, Kinsey on my lap. We all hold hands to say grace, and Gramma adds at the end, 'And Lord, let us have many more times at Camp Meeting, if it is Your will, Amen.' She tucks a napkin under Grampa's chin.

Everyone begins passing food around. Out of the corner of my eye, I see Taylor Witherspoon sauntering past and looking to see if I'm looking at him. I *am* looking at him, and smile to let him know that I like his looking at me. Mumma and Jody are giggling over some private joke. I help myself to more barbecue. It's good; sweet and spicy all at the same time. I chew for a long time, just absorbing the taste of it. From the next tent, we can hear music. Elvis Presley, singing *The Wonder of You* . . .

'Pass me more of that slaw. It's awful good.'
'Honey, who's that boy out there? He keeps looking over.'
'Anyone want some cornbread? It's fresh made.'
'Jenny? Where's Jenny?'
'Right here, Frank.'

Further reading

You can read this story and others by Carolyn Steele Agosta on the Internet. Visit her website, http://www.carolynagosta.com, for links.

When Ma and Pa Kept Control
by Thea Thompson

> Family life was very different 100 years ago in 1908. Edwardians would no doubt be shocked rigid if they could see us today . . .

This article is based on taped interviews carried out by members of the Department of Sociology, Essex University, in which elderly people recalled what it was like to be either a parent or a child 100 years ago.

No notions of family democracy or children's liberation troubled Edwardian parents. An unwritten contract operated, much like that between master and servant. Parents provided food, clothing and shelter as best they could: in return, children owed respect and unquestioning obedience until they set up homes of their own. Parents of all classes equally demanded respect. A London packing-case maker recalled that he wanted his children to behave 'in a deferential[1] sort of a way, you know. We've got to be respected', and a Nottingham man put a typical view, 'They was your father and mother – you respected them as mother and father, aye.'

Although providing for the family was primarily the parents' job, they did not consider it wrong, in hard times, to ask the children to help. Many children did not need to be asked, but found their own pennies in the many ways then open to them before they left school: catching rats for twopence each, selling postcards at the Liverpool docks at a penny for six, running errands, cab ducking,[2] scrubbing steps, minding babies. At 13 or 14 these children would expect to hand over their first full-time earnings – usually about 5s a week – to their parents, getting perhaps 1d or 2d back.

---

[1] **deferential**   respectful
[2] **cab ducking**   calling cabs for people

Decency, respectability and cleanliness – these, with honesty, were the virtues most parents tried to inculcate[3] as their part of the contract. There was not much time and energy, even given the inclination, to provide more spiritual frills. That was left to the Sunday school teachers and, to a lesser extent, the elementary school. Middle-class parents were not such solid supporters of Sunday school. They preferred to give their children religious instruction themselves, and their larger houses and their servants gave them more respite[4] from their children's company – one of the uses of Sunday school was to give parents a little privacy on Sunday afternoons.

How far was affection considered a parental duty? The relationship between a parent and a sick child would usually be tender. Much love and care was devoted to children in those days before antibiotics, when childhood illness could be very serious – diphtheria[5] was still common – and careful, patient nursing all parents could give. Babies, too, before they could toddle were not disciplined, and brothers and sisters would notice the affection and interest that the current baby attracted. Many mothers breast-fed for a year, in some cases even two, and recall the pleasure of nursing. Mrs Carter had seven children. She remembered:

When they was born I used to cuddle them up – 'cause you can love them then, can't you? When they got bigger – well . . . And when they got married – well they don't belong to you.

Yet many parents, despite long hours at work in the home and outside, could find time to be close to their children when they were no longer babies. A Wiltshire cowman's son remembered his relationship with his father, a widower:

We was one; him and me was one. I'd always go to him with any troubles, and he used to listen and if he could help he did and when we

---

[3]**inculcate**   teach by repetition
[4]**respite**   a rest
[5]**diphtheria**   an infectious disease causing breathing problems

sit on the couch like we did (we had a big old-fashioned sofa) he used to put his arm all round my shoulders. We used to sit there sometimes of an evening all cuddled up to him.

A Staffordshire boilermaker's daughter, one of seven children, said:

I used to like those Sundays best. We used to all draw round the fire on Sunday afternoon and talk about things, and if we couldn't find anything to talk about, we used to say, 'Mum, if we'd got enough money. could we have a shop?', and she'd say, 'Yes, what sort of a shop would you like?' and we'd go to work, see, and everybody'd have a different tale to tell about the shop we were going to have.

When mothers of nine or more children had to work full-time as well – . . . making shirts in London at 2s 9d a dozen, working in a Bradford mill from 6.30 am to 5.30 pm – a great deal of work fell on their daughters, particularly the older ones.

Unlike their brothers, who although they worked hard at getting money often had the fun and companionship of other boys, these girls working closely with their mothers had no time to go out and felt particularly deprived. And when the mother felt that the father was not helping enough financially, spending his money in the pub, her resentment shut her off even more from her children. Mrs Fletcher remembered her mother

frustrated, you know, with so many children. You couldn't talk to my mother, no. I can remember praying, this is the truth, if God would make me ill so my mother would talk to me and kiss me and have a little affection. Father? Oh hail fellow well met. 'You're all right, go on.' He was never a hard man. He couldn't be bothered really.

And yet too many children and too little money and time cannot have been the only factors inhibiting the flow of affection from mother to child. In families of three children or fewer, and in well-to-do families, some parents are also remembered as reserved and unapproachable, sometimes going so far as to repulse a caress or hug.

Middle-class girls sometimes seem to have received little show of affection from their mothers, often then feeling closer to their fathers. Mrs Lane, whose father was a successful wholesale merchant, remembered that he

was the gentler of the two and easygoing. He was never nasty. Mother could maybe be sarcastic, but Father was gentle. In fact I wasn't terribly fond of Mother, why I don't know. She was an ideal mother, but Father was a warmer and . . . I don't know what it was. He was a kindly man.

Not all children accepted their role as subordinates. Boys, particularly in urban slums, remember chafing[6] at restrictions, and several parents remember rebellious girls, particularly the youngest in small families. But insubordination[7] was not usually difficult to put down, as Mr Longton, manager in a Liverpool grocer's shop, found.

I only hit my youngest lad once. They never had a real thrashing, and the only time it was, he brushed some bread on the floor and I said, 'Pick it up.' And he wouldn't. And I made him pick it up because I knew I had to be master. But they never got a thrashing otherwise.

So universal was the belief that children should respect and obey parents that many children remember being given corporal punishment only once. A significant minority, mainly in rural families, recall childhood free from any punishment at all: 'We knew when Dad spoke that was it. They never laid a hand on us.'

But the absence of resort to punishment was not permissiveness. Obedience was enforced while the child remained under the parental roof. With certain exceptions, girls were expected to be home by 10 o'clock (9 o'clock on Sundays) and some parents insisted on earlier hours. Courting boyfriends were expected to leave at the time decreed and to bring the girlfriend back to her parents in time.

---

[6]**chafing** feeling irritated
[7]**insubordination** defiance

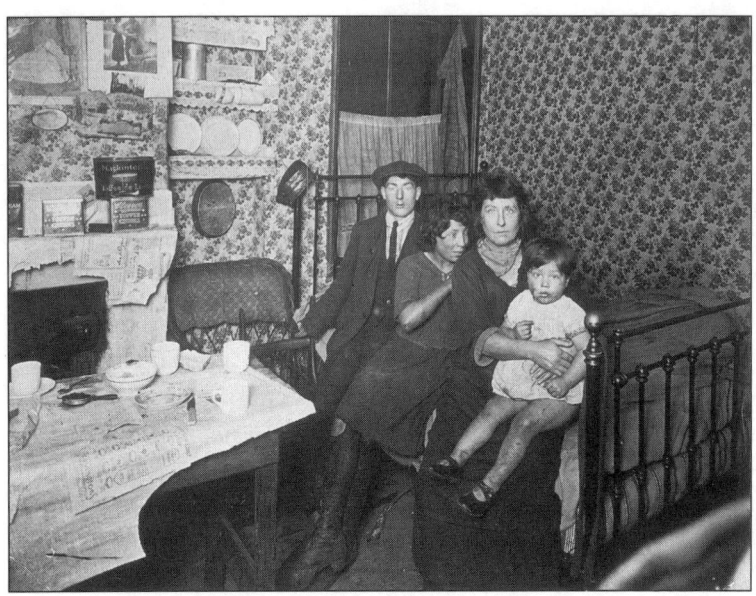

An Edwardian working-class family.

Me father told me husband – well, he was me young man at that time – 'Our bed time's 10 o'clock' – and it was sort of like it or lump it. He said to me, 'I can take the hint' and half-past nine he used to say 'It's our bed time', and that were it. Me husband daren't keep me about[8] because me father'd brought house down.

Mrs Halsell remembered how her usually mild father reacted when at the age of 17 she came in from the pictures half an hour after her regulation 9 o'clock curfew:

'I'll give you 10 o'clock at night! Get up those stairs – you go out no more this week.' And I was so surprised when he hit me with his slipper that I turned round and got another one.

Sons might be allowed a little more freedom but their fathers would usually ask when they expected to be in. Mr James, a clerk, was given a door key when he was 21 but told: 'Remember this is your home and don't abuse it.' But Mr Castle

---

[8]**about** near

when in his twenties, although he had been to university and was working, found his parents waiting up until 2 or 3 in the morning if he didn't let them know that he was coming home later than 11 o'clock.

And this was always a bit difficult because I'd lost my teetotal principles at this time, and going home occasionally and holding one's breath and talking through the side of one's mouth so one didn't breathe on anybody and so forth, occasionally created difficulties. Do you know, to the day of my father's death I daren't have told him that I took a drink – daren't is not the word – I wouldn't have hurt him by letting him know.

For some Edwardians the habits of filial[9] duty lasted for the whole of their lifetime.

Further reading

This period of history often gets forgotten but it was a time of great change and in many ways 'The Birth of Now'. Find out about the BBC series with this title on the website http://www.bbc.co.uk. You will also find plenty of fascinating facts at http://www.channel4.com/history: search for *The Edwardian Country House*.

You might also enjoy the *Flambards* trilogy by K. M. Peyton (Penguin Books Ltd, 1980), which is set in this period, or *The Ragged Trousered Philanthropist* by Robert Tressell (Oxford University Press, 2005), which is about Edwardian working-class hardship.

---

[9] **filial** son or daughter's

The Kitchen

by David Almond

> *The Kitchen* comes from *Counting Stars* (Hodder Children's Books, 2007), David Almond's collection of stories about growing up in a large Catholic family. It is a mixture of memory and dream, real and imaginary, as he remembers the deaths in his close family.

The drone of the distant city, the clatter and hum of Felling nearby. In another garden, children sing a skipping song: *January, February, March, April, May* . . . An invisible lark high above. A blackbird calling from the apple tree. The scent of roses and warm grass. The sun burns at the centre of the sky. Light pours down into the garden, through the window, through the gap of the half-open door, through dust that seethes, dances, glitters . . .

And Mam smiles.

'Hm. Just look at us. Right out of space again.'

Here she is on the old white chair with a hundred holes like stars. And Dad on the low stool at her side.

'We'd have moved on to a bigger place,' he says.

'I know,' she answers. 'Yes. I know.'

And here we are, leaning against the worktops, the fridge, the sink, the little table. We drink tea and eat toast. We allow the toast to cool for a moment, so that the butter we spread melts only at its edges, so that much of it remains, bright yellow, half-solid on the crisp surface. There is cheese, lemon curd, Golden Shred. So simple, so sweet, enough for all of us.

We breathe so gently, so carefully. We don't stare. The light pours in.

Barbara wears cream trousers, a white blouse, white shoes. Her hair is cut short but it curls around her ears, it curls on her brow. Little silver earrings like teardrops. A narrow silver necklace. She stands with her left hand resting on the bench and her head tilted languidly to one side. She is so shy here, with us all around her. She keeps lowering her eyes, and her face colours gently as she smiles.

I look at Mam and she shakes her head and bites her lip: just give her time. We don't stare. The light doesn't change, the singing goes on. Catherine catches my eye.

'Nothing must happen,' she says. 'Nothing.'

Dad touches Margaret's hand.

'I was thinking,' he says. 'Do you remember? One day you said to me, Where's the smallest place in the world?'

She shakes her head.

'I don't remember,' she whispers.

'You were young.'

He smiles at Margaret and at the memory of Margaret and for a moment we all see her as she was and as we were.

'I was thinking, Maybe this is it. Maybe this is the smallest place in the world. Just enough for all of us.'

'What happened?' says Margaret. 'Tell me about the day I asked you and what you said to me.'

'It was nothing much. You were on the floor with your head in the sideboard cupboard. I watched you climbing right inside. What you after? I said. I've lost Nancy in here, you said. The cupboard's too small to be lost in, I said. But she's so small, you said. I found the doll beside me on the settee. Here she is! I said. You ticked her off. Who said you could go off wandering all alone? you said. You came and sat on my knee and we looked at the open sideboard door and the dark cupboard. Could I have got lost in there? you said. Too small, I told you. You'd hardly get *in* it, never mind get lost in it. Look at the size of you and the size of that. We sat quiet for a while. The day was like this. Sun shining, blackbirds singing. After a while, you said, Where's the smallest place in the world? Then you said, What would we find sitting all safe inside?'

'What did you say?' says Margaret.

'Isn't it silly?' He smiles. 'I don't remember. But maybe this is it, this kitchen, and here we are, all sitting safe inside.'

Unchanging light, unchanging song: the lark, the blackbird, the children. The dust seethes and dances in the light.

Catherine takes more toast from beneath the grill. We allow it to cool for a moment before putting the butter on.

'This one got lost,' says Mam. 'Went off wandering on her own, the smallest of us all. Who said you could do that, now?'

Barbara blushes and smiles.

'That was the smallest place,' she whispers. 'No room for anybody else but me in there.'

'I know,' says Mam. 'Oh, I know.'

'Thought you'd all forsaken me. Thought you'd all forget me.'

'I wasn't even here when you were here,' says Mary. 'But I still remember you. I still don't forget you.'

'I know that now,' says Barbara. 'But I thought I'd be alone for ever. Me so little and all of you so big. And so many of you, more of you even though I was gone. You'd have each other and the little memory of me would just get lost.'

'We never forgot,' says Dad. 'And if we didn't remember true, we just made bits up.'

Barbara laughs.

'Made bits up!'

'Yes. Truth and memories and dreams and bits made up.'

'Bits made up. But bits made up that kept me safe and real in all your hearts.'

We listen to the beating of our hearts.

Barbara says, 'When I began to understand, I used to come among you. I knew you knew I was there. I knew you knew I was always there.'

'Yes,' says Mam. 'We always knew.'

We smile at her. We listen to the blackbirds, to the children singing.

'Tell us about another day,' says Mary.

'Tell them about another day,' says Dad.

'We were at the beach,' says Mam. She touches Barbara. 'All of us but you. South Shields, another day like this, all burning bright. Dad and I sat by the bandstand and spread the blankets and towels on the grass. Mary and Margaret were on their hunkers[1] at the sea's edge with their buckets, pouring sand into the sea and sea into the sand. Catherine knelt building a castle. The boys were right in, diving and swimming and yelling at the cold. We sat on the warm grass and leaned back on the warm bricks. Dad put a kettle on the primus.[2] We saw the fret[3] coming in. It was white and thick and so sudden. The horizon disappeared, then the great boat that was waiting to enter the Tyne, then the waves. And the fret came closer, until the boys were gone. You remember?'

'I remember,' says Dad. 'I ran down, and I called and called. I ran into the sea. The sea was icy cold and the air was icy cold. I stood there splashing, calling. You remember?'

'Yes,' says Colin. 'We heard you shouting and it was like you were a hundred miles away.'

'I stood up and watched,' says Mam. 'Dad in his soaking trousers, the girls behind him on the shore. I saw Dad running into the fret until he had disappeared, too.'

Dad laughs.

'Blundered into them, knocked them flying, tumbled into the sea myself. We came out icy cold and soaking wet.'

'Giggling and splashing,' says Mam. 'You all came up to me, to the bandstand, the tea, the sandwiches. Soon everybody wrapped in towels. You'll catch your deaths, I said. You will. You'll catch your deaths.'

We drink tea, nibble toast, try to remember.

'It was me that saw her,' says Catherine. 'The little girl standing in the fret, pale as the mist, knee-deep in the sea. I pointed. There! I said. There! We watched the fret, going back as quickly as it had come in. In the water, I said. There, in the fret. There. Peel your eyes. I ran down to the sea, pointing. There! The fret went back, the sea was empty, just water, little

---

[1] **on their hunkers**   squatting down
[2] **primus**   portable paraffin stove
[3] **fret**   a mist that forms at sea and moves inland with the incoming tide

waves. Not a soul in there. Dreamed it night after night. Little girl in the water. The missing one, the one who seemed always to be somewhere in the fringes. Catch her in the corner of your eye, then turn your head and she'd be gone.'

We turn our eyes to Barbara. She turns her eyes to each of us, eyes shining like the sea, complexion pale as sea fret.

'I didn't make you up,' says Catherine.

'No,' says Barbara, and she reaches out and touches Catherine's cheek. 'And it doesn't matter exactly what's true and what's made up. I was always there. I am always there, despite my death.'

We are silent at the word, but we sigh together, those of us who are in life and those of us who are in death.

'What's death?' says Mary suddenly. Mary looks at Mam, at Dad, at Barbara. 'You all died. What's death?'

'Death is very big and very frightening,' says Barbara. 'Death is being all alone and waiting for others to come to you.'

'Death is separation,' says Dad. 'It's when you're torn away from those who have hardly known you, and who will have trouble in remembering you.' He touches Mary on the cheek. 'Like you and Margaret,' he says. 'You would always have difficulty in remembering me.'

'Death is knowing you're about to die,' says Mam. 'It's seeing the dead and seeing the living all at once. It's wanting not to die and not to live. It's wanting to stay with the last breath when the dead and the living are all around you, and touching you, and whispering, It's all right, Mam. Everything's all right. But there's no way of staying with the last breath. You have to die.'

'And then?' says Colin. 'What happens then?'

Barbara smiles.

'And then the dead get together and tell stories about the living, just as the living tell stories about the dead.'

'Yes,' says Dad. 'The dead begin with, Do you remember? or, Let me tell you about the time, or, There was once . . .'

We're silent again. We listen to the birds, the children singing outside.

Mam laughs.

'I sang that,' she says. *'January, February, March, April . . .* Jumping the rope, running round to the line again. Time and again and time and again and time and again. There was once a little girl with lovely leaping legs . . . '

She hums the relentless tune and taps her toes on the floor.

'And anyway,' she says. 'As well as life and death, there's this.'

'What's this?' says Mary.

'The kitchen. Just the kitchen, I suppose.'

'The smallest place in the world,' says Dad. 'An impossible place. An impossible story. A kind of Heaven.'

'And what's Heaven?' says Colin.

'Maybe it's just this, an impossible afternoon when everyone is together all at once.'

We gaze out at the light, through the seething dust. The sun still hangs at the dead centre of the sky. The children and the blackbird sing. No one speaks. Nothing happens. We look at each other, touch each other.

'Tell us a story,' says Margaret.

'Tell us a story,' we say.

'There was once . . . ' says Mam.

We look at her.

'Yes,' she whispers. 'Listen. This is true . . . Hm. There was once a little boy from Carlisle Street who lost his voice in the winter snow. You remember?'

'I remember,' says Dad.

'His name was Jack Law,' says Mam. 'He had seven sisters, a loving mammy and a loving daddy, and nowt but sacking tied around his feet . . . '

We listen to the truth, the memories, the bits made up. We gaze at each other. We eat warm buttered toast. We know that the sun will fall, that the children and the birds will be silent. We know that we will return to separate lives and separate deaths. We listen to the stories, that for an impossible afternoon hold back the coming dark.

Further reading

All David Almond's books have a strange kind of magic about them. If you enjoyed this story, try *Skellig* (Hodder Children's Books, 2007), a wonderful novel about a boy who finds an angel in the garage.

Patterned Ways
by Jo Hilton

> This poem and the two that follow are concerned with life going on over generations. Two were written relatively recently, one over 100 years ago. Can you tell which is the oldest?

I shall walk in my father's steps,
Not because it is easy,
But because I like the deep marks
He always makes. They are easy to follow,
Whether I trudge behind him in the snow,
Through high tall grasses, along the dunes,
Or follow him through his ploughed furrows.

When I was small, I had to stretch
My legs to match his stride.
Sometimes I failed,
But always I tried.

He shows no sign,
    nor has he ever shown a sign
He is aware of this, my following;
He sets his patterned mark for me
And filled with pride, I bravely follow him.

Now having grown a bit,
    I tread behind
With ease. Occasionally,
    (unless I watch myself),
I walk with even longer stride

And over-reach his tracks,
Make new ones of my own.

God grant that I shall mark
    a patterned way
As clear for my own son.

Further reading

Jo Hilton's poem comes from an interesting collection called *All in the Family* (Oxford University Press, 1999), edited by John Foster.

Follower

by Seamus Heaney

> Like *Patterned Ways*, this poem is about following in parents' footsteps, literally and figuratively.

My father worked with a horse-plough,
His shoulders globed like a full sail strung
Between the shafts and the furrow.[1]
The horses strained at his clicking tongue.

An expert. He would set the wing
And fit the bright steel-pointed sock.
The sod[2] rolled over without breaking.
At the headrig,[3] with a single pluck

An expert.

---

[1]**furrow** a long narrow trench made by a plough
[2]**sod** earth
[3]**headrig** the top of the field, end of the furrow

Of reins, the sweating team turned round
And back into the land. His eye
Narrowed and angled at the ground,
Mapping the furrow exactly.

I stumbled in his hob-nailed wake,
Fell sometimes on the polished sod;
Sometimes he rode me on his back
Dipping and rising to his plod.

I wanted to grow up and plough,
To close one eye, stiffen my arm.
All I ever did was follow
In his broad shadow round the farm.

I was a nuisance, tripping, falling,
Yapping always. But today
It is my father who keeps stumbling
Behind me, and will not go away.

Further reading

Seamus Heaney has published many collections of verse and many of his poems are about his Irish farming family. If you enjoyed this poem, try *Digging* or *Picking Blackberries*. You can read both at http://www. poemhunter.com.

Heredity
by Thomas Hardy

> This poem is concerned with physical family likeness. The title, *Heredity*, means the passing-on of genetic characteristics from parents to their children.

I am the family face;
Flesh perishes, I live on,
Projecting trait and trace
Through time to times anon,
And leaping from place to place
Over oblivion.

The years-heired feature that can
In curve and voice and eye
Despise the human span
Of durance – that is I;
The eternal thing in man,
That heeds no call to die.

Further reading

Thomas Hardy is probably most famous as a novelist. Several of his novels have been made into films, including *Far from the Madding Crowd* (Warner Home Video, 2004) and *Tess of the D'Urbervilles* (as *Tess*, produced by Uca, 2007). Some of his poems you might enjoy – you'll find them in anthologies such as *The Puffin Book of Classic Verse* (Puffin Books, 1997) – include *The Convergence of the Twain*, about the sinking of the *Titanic*, and *I Look into My Glass*.

Activities

Two poems and *From the Grave to the Cradle*

Before you read

1 What is a family tree, and why is it called that? Do you know anything about your own family tree? Use the illustration on page 191 to help you draw yours. Leave blanks for people you don't know. You could ask for more information at home.

2 What do you know already about Anglo-Saxon family life? Pool your knowledge with a partner.

What's it about?

Work with a partner to answer questions 3 to 5.

3 a In *Beginnings*, who are 'one', 'two', and ' three'?
  b Why did the howl of the wind become a song? And how do things get better?

4 In *Family Tree*, what are the young branches? How do the roots still feed them?

5 In *From the Grave to the Cradle*, why do you think people buried objects with the dead?

Thinking about the text

6 Can you tell that *Beginnings* and *Family Tree* are both by the same person? What do they have in common? Look at:
   - line arrangement
   - use of italics
   - theme.

   How do the two poems link with *From the Grave to the Cradle*? Write a paragraph or two detailing the similarities between all three texts.

7 Imagine that you're a journalist on the local paper, and write an article about the archaeological discovery in *From the Grave to the Cradle*. Think of an attention-grabbing headline, and remember the journalists' rule of five Ws – who, what, where, when, why.

8 Write a time travel story in which you visit a Neolithic or Anglo-Saxon family. What would be the biggest shock for a modern character? Would there have been pleasures too?

Little Brother

Before you read

1 What do you know already about country life in Victorian times? Use library books or the Internet to research some background which you could present to the rest of your class or group.

What's it about?

Read the text and answer questions 2 to 4 by yourself. Then compare your answers with a partner's.

2 Why does the narrator think it's a mercy that the baby was born dead?

3 Why isn't Mr Hodd with his wife? What do you think she feels about his absence?

4 How is the boy working with his father 'the eldest hope'?

Thinking about the text

5 Put Mrs Hodd in the hot seat and question her about her family and situation. Think about these questions as you prepare.
   - Is the baby 'desecrated', or is Mrs Hodd right to defend her children?
   - Was it irresponsible of the Hodds to bring so many children into the world when they couldn't afford to feed them?
   - Who do you think is to blame for their situation?

6 What do you think the writer feels towards the Hodd family? Look carefully at the descriptive language she uses and make a list of examples that convey her attitude.

7 Write a short paragraph describing how you reacted when you found out about the doll. How does the writer create the sense of shock?

Keeping Mum

Before you read

1 Do you have any 'extraordinary/ordinary tales' about your family? Are there any anecdotes that are told over and over? Share your stories in a small group.

2 Have you seen either of your parents very upset? Did you know what was wrong? If you feel happy to share the experience, talk with a partner.

What's it about?

Read the text and answer questions 3 to 5 by yourself. Then compare your answers with a partner's.

3 In what way was the writer's father an 'integrated Asian', and in what way was he not quite?

4 How did the writer gain her father's affection?

5 What upset her father when she was taken to hospital?

Thinking about the text

6 Write a short personal response to this story. Use the following questions to help you:
- What did you like/dislike about the story?
- What is the double meaning of the title?
- What is the mood of this account? Is it happy or tragic? Pick out three words or phrases that convey the mood to you. Explain your choice.

7 What qualities or achievements help you to gain your parents' approval? Write a short piece of personal writing.

Oral Tradition

Before you read

1 Talk in a small group about any holiday traditions you have in your families. Who goes on holiday together? Are grandparents included?

What's it about?

Read the text and answer questions 2 to 4 by yourself. Then compare your answers with a partner's.

2 Why does Gramma have to be away from her husband? How can you tell that Gramma and Grampa had a happy marriage?

3 What makes Gramma such good company? Collect words and phrases from the text which convey her personality.

4 Draw a family tree, starting with Gramma and Grampa, showing all the members of the writer's family.

Thinking about the text

5 The narrator says: 'boys have more interesting lives'. Was that true then? Is it true now? Have a debate in your class or group.

6 Write your own story about a holiday where the young are beginning a relationship as the old are coming to the end of one.

7 Look carefully at the techniques the writer uses to build up atmosphere. Find examples of:
- descriptions of the weather and how that relates to inner feelings
- vivid details describing the setting
- use of dialogue and action to convey character.

Then write an essay analysing these effects, and describing your response to the story.

When Ma and Pa Kept Control

Before you read

1 Do your parents or grandparents ever say 'We were never allowed to speak to our parents like that' or 'We weren't allowed to pick and choose what we ate' and so on? In a small group, brainstorm some of the main differences you are aware of between child/parent relationships now and when your grandparents were kids.

What's it about?

Read the article and answer questions 2 and 3 by yourself. Then compare your answers with a partner's.

2 How were children expected to behave towards their parents 100 years ago? Make a list of Edwardian rules.

3 What do you think were some of the advantages of family life then? And what would you personally find hardest to bear? Make some notes to discuss with your partner.

Thinking about the text

4 Make a list of your family rules to compare with the list of Edwardian rules. Would you say you were 'deferential'?

5 What do the direct quotations in italics add to the article? How does the language differ from the main text? Make a list of some of the words and phrases that belong to oral rather than written language and then write a short essay about the article, comparing the two styles.

6 Write two scenes, showing a typical family Sunday in Edwardian times and today, called 'Then and Now'. Use information from the text and your own experience or imagination. You could develop this into a performance for your class.

The Kitchen

Before you read

1 What images, feelings or memories does your family kitchen hold for you? Make notes to share with the class or small group.

What's it about?

This is a mysterious story which may take a while for you to understand. Don't give up!

2 Read the story again and discuss it with a partner. Make a list together of some of the things you find puzzling. Work out who is dead and who is alive. Then answer the questions below.

3 Where do you think the kitchen is? What clues are there that it isn't as ordinary as it might seem? Discuss them with your partner.

4 In the introduction, David Almond says that his stories are partly 'an attempt to rediscover what is lost'. What is he rediscovering in this story? And how do you think it 'holds back the coming of the dark'? Discuss your ideas with your partner.

Thinking about the text

5 Write a paragraph or two explaining how the writer builds up the strange atmosphere of magic in the story. Look particularly at:
- his use of the senses (sound, smell and sight)
- the pattern of the dialogue
- the effect of varied sentence length.

6 Several of the characters describe what they think death is. Do you agree with any of them? Or do you have other views of your own? Write a paragraph in which you set out your opinion.

7 Imagine you are writing a short review for the school library to tell others about this story. Remember to answer the following questions:
- What's it about?
- What's the setting?
- What are the characters like?
- What do you especially like/dislike?
- Who would you recommend it to?

Patterned Ways, *Follower* and *Heredity*

Before you read

For questions 1 and 2, discuss your ideas in a small group.

1 Are there any ways in which you follow in your family's footsteps?

2 Do your relations comment on family likenesses: 'You've got your father's nose / mother's smile' and so on? Who do you think you look like?

What's it about?

Work with a partner to answer questions 3 and 4.

3 Read through all three poems. Then read them aloud to each other. Note any words or phrases that puzzle you, or that you particularly like. Discuss first impressions: which poem strikes you the most strongly?

4 Try to explain the linked themes of the poems in a single sentence.

Thinking about the text

5 Write a paragraph or two comparing Hilton's and Heaney's feelings about following their fathers, and their reaction when the position changes. Support your opinions with quotes from the texts.

6 Is a sense of heredity, of family likeness, or following in parents' footsteps, important to you? Why / why not? Are there other 'eternal things' you believe in or value? How would you like to be remembered after your death? Discuss your ideas in a small group.

7 Write a short essay comparing these three poems, bringing out the similarity of the themes. Are there any differences you notice? Which do you prefer and why? Use your discussion notes to help you. Think about:
- rhyme and rhythm and other poetic devices
- language (Hardy's poem was written over 100 years ago and Heaney's describes an old method of farming)
- the overall mood or tone.

Compare and contrast

1. Write a comparison of the three short stories in this section, *The Kitchen*, *Oral Tradition* and *Little Brother*. Think about:
   - plot/theme
   - characters
   - setting
   - mood
   - style.

   Which do you prefer, and why?

2. Which text from this section stays in your mind, either because you liked it or because it irritated or bored you in some way? Write a paragraph or two explaining your reactions, quoting examples from the text.

3. Several of the pieces in this section are about life carrying on from one generation to the next. Write a short story of your own with this theme. It could be based on your own experience or entirely imaginary.

4. Think about the anonymous child's grave in *From the Grave to the Cradle*. Have a go at writing a poem modelled on Thomas Hardy's, beginning 'I am the nameless child'.

5. Think back over all the pieces you have read in this anthology. Choose one character who you would like to have in your family, and one character you wouldn't. Write two 'pen portraits' (descriptions).

6. There are inevitable overlaps between the four sections, and many pieces would fit happily into more than one section. Which texts do you think could have been placed elsewhere? Discuss your ideas in a small group and make notes so that you can report back to the rest of your class. Don't forget to explain your reasoning.

Notes on authors

Carolyn Steele Agosta is an American writer whose stories have been published in print and online. Find out more about her on her website: http://www.carolynagosta.com

David Almond (1951–) was born in Newcastle and now lives in Northumberland with his family. His first novel for young people, *Skellig*, was published in 1998. He also writes for the theatre. His website (http://www.davidalmond.com) includes writing tips as well as information about his life and work.

Rachel Anderson (1943–) has written widely for children and young people. Three of her most popular novels are *The War Orphan* (1984), *Warlands* (2000) and *The Poacher's Son* (1982). When she's not writing she is involved in working for children with special needs. She has a website at http://www.rachelanderson.co.uk

Kiran Ansari is an American Muslim writer who publishes articles in print and online on, amongst other topics, parenting and faith. She has an extensive website at http://www.kiranansari.com

Elizabeth Baines was born in Wales and lives in Manchester. She has been a teacher and an actor as well as a prize-winning writer of fiction and drama. Find out more at http://www.e.baines.zen.co.uk

The Beatles are probably the most famous pop group ever. Formed around 1960, the 'fab four' – John Lennon, Paul McCartney, George Harrison and Ringo Starr – had a lasting influence on British culture. Their lyrics have even appeared on exam papers!

Elizabeth Bennett is an American poet living in Virginia. Her poems have appeared in many American literary journals and she contributed to the anthology, *When I Am an Old Woman I Shall Wear Purple* (1987).

Richard Benson (1966–) grew up on a farm in Yorkshire. After a childhood spent crashing tractors, he left home to become a journalist. *The Farm* is his first book and was shortlisted for a Richard and Judy Book Club award.

Chris Buckton (1936–) is a children's writer who has been involved in education for over 30 years. She was awarded an MBE in 1999 for services to children's literacy.

Lynette Craig (1949–) was born in Birmingham. After working as a teacher she took an MPhil course in writing at Glamorgan University. She writes poetry for children and adults.

David Crystal (1941–) is a world-famous language expert and author of important books on the history of the English language. He was awarded an OBE in 1995. As well as his academic publications he writes popular books on language usage, including *By Hook or by Crook* (HarperPress, 2007). He has a blog at http://david-crystal.blogspot.com

Hugh Cunningham is Professor of Social History at the University of Kent. He has published several books on the life of children through the ages, including the book to accompany the radio series, *The Invention of Childhood* (BBC Books, 2006).

Charles Dickens (1812–70) is one of Britain's greatest writers. Born into a poor family, he soon became celebrated as a popular novelist. His stories created unforgettable characters, as well as helping to change some of the injustices in Victorian society.

Anne Fine (1947–) was born and educated in the Midlands, and now lives in County Durham. She has written numerous highly acclaimed prize-winning books for children and adults. She was appointed Children's Laureate in 2001. Visit her website at http://www.annefine.co.uk

Anne Frank (1929–45) was a Jewish girl born in Germany. The family moved to Amsterdam in 1933 after the Nazis gained power in Germany. They lived in hiding to escape persecution, but were betrayed in 1944 and sent to concentration camps. Anne Frank died of typhus shortly after her imprisonment. Her diary still lives on. The house the Franks hid in is now a museum (http://www.annefrank.org).

Adèle Geras (1944–) was born in Jerusalem. She was educated in England and now lives in Manchester with her family. She has written over 90 books for children and adults. She has a website at http://www.adelegeras.com

Nadine Gordimer (1923–) was born and lives in South Africa. She won the Nobel Prize for Literature in 1991 and has written numerous novels and short stories.

Lee Hall (1966–) was born and brought up in Newcastle. He studied at Cambridge University and then worked in youth theatre. He has written award-winning plays for radio, many of which are collected in two volumes, *Plays: 1* (2002) and *Plays: 2* (2004).

Thomas Hardy (1840–1928) was born in Dorset and returned there after some years in London. His first poems were rejected, but he achieved fame through his novels, mostly set in the Dorset countryside. When *Jude the Obscure* (1895) received critical reviews, he turned to poetry again, writing some of his most successful work in his 70s.

Jeremy Hart is a freelance journalist. He writes for the *Sunday Times* and the BBC's *Top Gear* magazine, amongst other publications.

Seamus Heaney (1939–) was born on a farm in Ireland, where he was educated. He began to write when he got his first teaching job in Belfast. He now lives and writes in the Irish Republic as well as teaching regularly in America. In 1995 he was awarded the Nobel Prize for Literature.

Jo Hilton's poem *Patterned Ways* was contributed to John Foster's anthology, *All in the Family* (1994), through a link with the Swanwick Writers' Summer School – a well-known school for budding writers.

Elizabeth Jolley (1923–2007) was born in Birmingham. In 1959 she emigrated to Western Australia where she had a variety of jobs before becoming well known as a writer in her 50s.

Jackie Kay (1961–) had a Scottish mother and a Nigerian father and was brought up in Glasgow by adoptive parents. She writes poetry for children and adults as well as novels and short stories. She lives in Manchester with her son.

Kit and the Widow describe themselves as 'two men and a piano'. The two men are Kit Hesketh-Harvey and Richard Sisson (the Widow). They have performed at the Edinburgh Fringe and in West End theatres, and on radio shows.

Mary Mann (1848–1929) was born in Norwich. She married a farmer and moved to the village of Shropham, where she was involved in visiting the sick and caring for other unfortunates among the poor agricultural labourers. These experiences inspired her stories, some of which are still in print.

Katherine Mansfield (1888–1923) was born in New Zealand, but after a lonely childhood she moved to England. After an unhappy marriage and a miscarriage she finally attracted notice through her short stories and in 1918 married the editor of a literary magazine, John Middleton Murry. But ill-health and depression still haunted her. She died of tuberculosis at the age of 35.

Annette Mbaye d'Erneville (1926–) was born in Senegal. She trained as a teacher and also worked as a reporter and magazine editor. She has written all her life, and has published prize-winning poetry and children's literature in French.

Adrian Mitchell (1932–) studied at Oxford University. He moved to London in the 1960s and worked as a freelance journalist, writing on pop music, books and television. He has written novels, poetry and plays. Find out more at http://www.rippingyarns.co.uk/adrian

Judith Nicholls (1941–) is one of Britain's best-known poets for children, with over 50 books published. Since 1985 she has visited more than 500 schools. She has also appeared on radio, on TV and in a poetry workshop with Michael Rosen.

Hiawyn Oram studied English and drama in South Africa before moving to Britain to work in advertising. Her writing career took off with some highly successful children's books, including the *Mona the Vampire* series and the popular picture books *Angry Arthur* (1982) and *Just Dog* (1998). She lives in South London and has two grown-up sons.

Sue Palmer (1948–) is a writer, broadcaster and education consultant. She is a popular speaker, and acts as an independent adviser to the Department of Education. She lives with her family in Cornwall.

Shyama Perera grew up in London in the 1960s, and works as a novelist, journalist and columnist. Her three novels are *Haven't Stopped Dancing Yet* (1999), *Bitter Sweet Symphony* (2000) and *Do the Right Thing* (2002).

Sara Selvarajah is a *Sunday Telegraph* reader whose contribution to the column *In Your Own Words* was chosen for the collection with the same title (Simon & Schuster Ltd, 2005).

William Shakespeare (c.1564–1616) has a unique reputation as perhaps the greatest writer of all time, although not much is known about his life. He was born in Stratford and probably moved to London around 1590 and worked in the theatre, acting as well as writing. He produced almost two plays a year, and wrote *Romeo and Juliet* in 1595. He spent his last years in Stratford.

Thea Thompson (1937–) wrote her article when she was a research assistant and fieldwork supervisor on a funded project called 'Family Life and Work Experience before 1918'. Four hundred and forty-four people born before 1905 were interviewed in England, Scotland and Wales about their experiences. She has also written a book on the same topic: *Edwardian Childhoods* (1981).

Acknowledgements

The volume editor and publishers acknowledge the following sources of copyright material and are grateful for the permissions granted. While every effort has been made, it has not always been possible to identify the sources of all the material used, or to trace all copyright holders. If any omissions are brought to our notice we will be happy to include the appropriate acknowledgements on reprinting.

p. 2: 'My House' by Annette Mbaye d'Erneville; p. 3: 'An Overcrowded House' by Adèle Geras © 1990 Adèle Geras, from *My Grandmother's Stories*, permission granted by the author; p. 10: 'Ramadan: Why Muslim Families Fast' by Kiran Ansari; p. 15: 'Our family mealtimes are battlegrounds' from *Family forum: Reader to reader: Your problems, your solutions: Our family mealtimes are battlegrounds*, Staff 07, October 2006, Copyright Guardian News & Media Ltd 2006; p. 19: 'A Gentleman's Agreement' from *Stories* by Elizabeth Jolley, copyright © Elizabeth Jolley; p. 26: 'My Parents' by Adrian Mitchell from *Ride the Nightmare* (Copyright © Adrian Mitchell 1971), reproduced by permission of PFD (www.pfd.co.uk) on behalf of Adrian Mitchell, (Adrian Mitchell Educational Health Warning! Adrian Mitchell asks that none of his poems be used in connection with any examinations whatsoever!); p. 29: 'Forging a Family' by Sue Palmer, from *Toxic Childhood* published by Orion Books, an imprint of The Orion Publishing Group; p. 39: 'The Trouble Was Meals' by Elizabeth Bennett; p. 50: 'Buried Treasure' from *The Giddy Limit* by Chris Buckton; p. 61: 'A Parents' and Teenagers' Alphabet Book' by David Crystal; p. 63: 'Urgent Note to My Parents' by Hiawyn Oram © 1993 Hiawyn Oram; p. 64: 'One Small Step' by Shyama Perera; p. 78: 'Independence' an extract from *The Diary of A Young Girl: The Definitive Edition* by Anne Frank, edited by Otto H Frank and Mirjam Pressler, translated by Susan Massotty (Viking, 1997) copyright © The Anne Frank-Fonds, Basle, Switzerland, 1991, English translation copyright © Doubleday a division of Bantam Doubleday Dell Publishing Group Inc, 1995; p. 83: 'Getting the Messages' by Anne Fine from *Very Different* published by Egmont / Mammoth; p. 93: 'Family Values' from *The Farm* by Richard Benson (Hamish Hamilton, 2005), Copyright © Richard Benson, 2005; p. 100: 'She's Leaving Home' lyrics by John Lennon / Paul McCartney © 1967 Sony / ATV Tunes LLC, administered by Sony / ATV Music Publishing (all rights reserved), used by permission; p. 102: Act 3 Scene 5 of *Romeo and Juliet* by William Shakespeare from Cambridge School Shakespeare series, edited by Rex Gibson, 2005, © Cambridge University Press, reproduced with permission; p. 118: 'Lost and Found' by Rachel Anderson © Rachel Anderson 2004; p. 122: 'A Family Photo' by Lynette Craig © Lynette Craig; p. 123: 'Two of Everything' from *Two's Company* by Jackie Kay (Blackie, 1992) Copyright © Jackie Kay, 1992; p. 124: 'Saturday Fathers' by Kit Hesketh Harvey; p. 126: 'New Families' from *Parent Problems! Children's views on life after parents have split up* edited by Bren Neale and Amanda Wade, published by Young Voice, 2000; p. 130: 'The Ultimate Safari' by Nadine Gordimer from *Jump and Other Stories*, published by Bloomsbury, with the permission of AP Watt Ltd on behalf of Felix Licensing BV, Copyright © Felix Licensing BV, 1991, reprinted by permission of Penguin Group (Canada); p. 142: 'Me, a mother at 15? No way!' by Jeremy Hart for *The Independent*, published in June 1997; p. 148: 'The Sorrows of Sandra Saint' from *Spoonface Steinberg and other plays* by Lee Hall, published by BBC Books, reprinted by permission of The Random House Group Ltd; p. 164: 'Compass and Torch' by Elizabeth Baines, extracted from *Balancing on the Edge of the World*, Salt (2007) © Elizabeth Baines; p. 190: Two poems, 'Beginnings' and 'Family Tree', by Judith Nicholls, © Judith Nicholls 1993, first published in *All In The Family*, compiled by John Foster, published by Oxford University Press, reprinted by permission of the author; p. 193: 'From the Grave to the Cradle' from *The Invention of Childhood* by Hugh Cunningham, published by BBC Books, reprinted by permission of The Random House Group Ltd; p. 202: 'Keeping Mum' by Sara Selvarajah from *In Your Own Words: Extraordinary Tales from Ordinary Life* published by Simon & Schuster, 2005; p. 204: 'Oral Tradition' by Carolyn Steele Agosta; p. 214: 'When Ma and Pa Kept Control' by Thea Thompson; p. 220: 'The Kitchen' by David Almond from *Counting Stars*, published by Hodder Childrens' Books © David Almond, reproduced by permission of Hodder and Stoughton Limited; p. 227: 'Patterned Ways' by Jo Hilton; p. 229: 'Follower' by Seamus Heaney, by permission of Faber and Faber Ltd.

The publishers would like to thank the following for permission to reproduce photographs: p. 13: Sally and Richard Greenhill / Alamy; p. 69: Charlie Phillips / Hulton Archive / Getty Images; p. 80: Anne

Frank-Fonds – Basel / Anne Frank House / Premium Archive / Getty Images; p. 94: vario images GmbH & Co.KG / Alamy; p. 119: Francoise De Mulder / Roger Viollet / Getty Images; p. 125: © Edward Bock / Corbis; p. 137: William F. Campbell / Time & Life Pictures / Getty Images; p. 169: imagebroker / Alamy; p. 176: RIBA Library Photographs Collection; p. 218: Photolibrary; p. 229: Hulton Archive / Getty Images.

The cartoons on pages 17, 18 and 195 are printed with permission of www.CartoonStock.com.